Sappho

ANCIENTS IN ACTION

Catullus
Amanda Hurley

Cleopatra
Susan Walker and Sally-Ann Ashton

Horace
Philip Hills

Lucretius
John Godwin

Ovid: love songs
Genevieve Liveley

Ovid: myth and metamorphosis
Sarah Annes Brown

Sappho
Marguerite Johnson

Spartacus
Theresa Urbainczyk

ANCIENTS IN ACTION

SAPPHO

Marguerite Johnson

BRISTOL CLASSICAL PRESS

First published in 2007 by
Gerald Duckworth & Co. Ltd.
90-93 Cowcross Street, London EC1M 6BF
Tel: 020 7490 7300
Fax: 020 7490 0080
inquiries@duckworth-publishers.co.uk
www.ducknet.co.uk

A catalogue record for this book is available
from the British Library

ISBN 1 85399 690 4
EAN 978185399 690 0

Typeset by e-type, Liverpool
Printed and bound in Great Britain by CPI Bath

Contents

For my sister, Kathleen, with love.

Acknowledgements and Conventions

I am grateful to the following for their comments on the draft of the manuscript: Frances Muecke (University of Sydney), Terry Ryan (University of Newcastle), and David McLean.

Colleagues at the University of Adelaide, particularly Jacqueline Clarke, were welcoming and supportive during my sabbatical stay there during October 2005.

Thank you also to Antony and Rebis Music for permission to use the lyrics from the album, *I am a bird now.*

All translations unless indicated otherwise are my own. Texts and emendations of Sappho are based on those by Denys Page (Clarendon Press: 1955) and D.A. Campbell (Harvard University Press: 1990).

*

In translations of Sappho's work, parentheses denote suggested emendations to partially illegible sections of the text; ellipses mark damaged parts of the text; and square brackets are used to facilitate the meaning where necessary.

Most of the references contained in the Notes are cited in the Select Bibliography, except for material dealing with textual issues, or topics of limited general interest to Sapphic studies per se.

Hope There's Someone

So here's hoping I will not drown
Or paralyze in light
And godsend I don't want to go
To the seal's watershed

Spiralling

Where go
where now
Can't stand
and if I can
Can't die
I'm freezing
Sly curse
I'm spiralling

Antony and the Johnsons,
© Rebis Music (2004)

Introduction

It is an auspicious event when a discovery is made that sheds new light on the world of ancient literature. It is especially propitious that in the year preceding the writing of this book a new papyrus was found that has contributed to the scarce remains of the poetry of Sappho. Researchers Michael Gronewald and Robert Daniel, working in the archives of Cologne University, discovered a document, dated to the third century BC and originally part of a mummy cartonnage,[1] which records quotations from three of Sappho's poems. The second quotation, when combined with a previously preserved fragment from Oxyrhynchus (found in 1922), resulted in a complete work, *poem* 58. In 2004 Gronewald and Daniel published two articles on the fragments in the academic journal *Zeitschrift für Papyrologie und Epigraphik*. Martin West then published the new poem in the original Greek with an English translation in the *Times Literary Supplement* on 21 June 2005, thus introducing the discovery to a wider audience.

Poem 58 tells of Sappho's emotional response to growing old and begins with an address to the young:

Be passionate for the beautiful gifts of the fragrant-breasted
    Muses,
o children, and for the clear, sweet-singing lyre.

Old age has now seized my once-tender body;
my hair has become light instead of dark;

9

my heart has grown heavy; my knees refuse to support me,
which once upon a time were as lithe for the dance as fawns.

I often mourn this state; but what am I to do?
There is no way, being human, not to grow old.

They say that rosy-armed Dawn, mad with love,
once carried Tithonus to the end of the world;

beautiful and youthful then, but in time grey age
engulfed him, he the husband of a goddess.

It is evident that Sappho's poetry speaks to us for the very
reason that she is capable – more than capable – of
succinctly conveying the human condition. The pain, both
emotional and physical, of growing old is suggested in the
advice addressed to adolescents to revel in the gifts of
artistic endeavour, here personified by the Muses, goddesses
who inspire music and poetry. In these opening lines, we
sense Sappho's sorrow at the passing of her own youth, the
impression being confirmed by lines 3-8 in which she
describes the ageing process and its effects. Sappho then
recalls the myth of Tithonus, the beautiful mortal who
became the object of desire of Dawn, goddess of the
morning light, who snatched him away to Olympus, home
of the gods, to live with her. As Sappho and her ancient
audience knew, the tale is a tragic one: Dawn, who ensured
Tithonus' eternal life, forgot to ensure eternal youth.
Horrified at his ageing body Dawn locked Tithonus away to
languish alone forever.

West observes that the fragment is resoundingly indicative
of Sappho's poetic skill: 'The poem is a small masterpiece:

simple, concise, perfectly formed, an honest, unpretentious expression of feeling, dignified in its restraint.'[2] Not everyone greeted the discovery with praise, however; Germaine Greer's reaction was: 'If Sappho wrote this kind of stuff, we can afford to be without her.'[3] This is a dramatic reappraisal for the scholar who, several years prior to this statement, endorsed Algernon Charles Swinburne's opinion that 'Sappho is simply nothing less – as she is certainly nothing more – than the greatest poet who ever was at all.'[4] It seems, nevertheless, that Greer is in the minority on this issue, with modern enthusiasm for the genius of Sappho, evidenced by the praise of West, matching the admiration of antiquity. In an epigram attributed to Plato (*c.* 427-348 BC), for example, she is referred to as the Tenth Muse:

> Some say there are nine Muses. How imprudent!
> Note well: Sappho of Lesbos is the tenth![5]

These lines indicate the respect the men of antiquity had for Sappho, which was somewhat unusual, since women did not earn admiration easily, except in the realms of beauty, chastity, motherhood and housekeeping.

There were also staunch male critics of Sappho and while none of them attacked her poetry, they certainly scrutinised her personal life. One example of this criticism is reflected in an anonymous biographical passage dating from the second or third century BC:

> Some have accused her of being irregular in her ways and a lover of women. In appearance she seems to have been contemptible and exceedingly ugly, being dark in complexion and of a considerably small stature.[6]

This extract reveals much about the ancient view of women who were reputed to be attracted to other women. Indeed males were able to court and become intimately involved with other males, while women who were inclined towards their own sex were generally vilified.

Likewise, the writers of the Roman age regularly revealed a preoccupation with Sappho's perceived sexuality and were decidedly disapproving. Horace (65-8 BC) in *Epistles* 1.19.28, for example, applies to Sappho the adjective *mascula* (masculine), on which Porphyrion (third century AD) offers two interpretations:

> 'Masculine Sappho,' either because she is celebrated for her poetry, in which men usually excel, or because she is criticised for having been a *tribas* (tribad).[7]

Context suggests that Horace was primarily referring to Sappho's skill as poet when he described her as *mascula*; he does, after all, cite her as a poetic model. Nevertheless, as Porphyrion suggests, there remains the other possibility, and we would be naïve to reject a credible *double entendre*.

As previously noted, women in antiquity were primarily praised in their roles as dutiful daughters, chaste wives and devoted mothers, and it is in this context that we should perhaps assess Horace's reference. Women were simply not expected or encouraged to compose, for this was primarily the domain of men. In fact, comparatively speaking, there were very few female authors in ancient Greece and Rome, a historical reality based largely on the lack of education offered to women. Not surprisingly, there are only approximately one hundred recorded names of female poets, of which around fifty are represented by extant material (essentially in fragmentary form).[8] Of these, Sappho appears to be the oldest and is certainly the most revered.[9]

Singing in the sixth century BC[10] on the Greek island of Lesbos off the coast of Turkey, Sappho may appear to the modern reader to be somewhat of an anomaly in view of the generally accepted tenet that the Greeks and Romans either excluded or limited female access to education. However, it seems Sappho was part of an 'enlightened' society that included women in the sphere of formal learning. The praise of Sappho as the Tenth Muse is indicative of her skills as a poet and her reputation as a poet's poet. A reading of her work in the original Aeolic dialect[11] – or in a translation that pays deference to her use of language – is testimony to the Tenth Muse hyperbole. That her skill was revered throughout antiquity and beyond speaks of a rigorous education as well as a considerable, natural artistic talent.

The exact nature of Sappho's education is, however, open to debate. Scholars know little about the formal instruction of women in antiquity, and all that can be assumed with some certainty is that Sappho, as a member of the upper echelon of society in the capital city of Lesbos, Mytilene, received an extensive education in choral composition and performance. It has long been posited that Sappho was a teacher at a school for girls that presumably had been modelled on something akin to the system in which she herself had been educated. Although there is little if any direct evidence for such a theory outside late biographical and literary accounts, some scholars still argue that it is not entirely misguided to think of Sappho as being connected in some way, formally or informally, to an all-female group. The nature of this is, however, open to debate. One theory is that Sappho was a member of a religious or cultic group, perhaps centred on the worship of the goddess Aphrodite (Venus in Rome), and in support of this, various pieces are cited. For example, *fragment 2*, in which Sappho writes of Cypris (Aphrodite),[12] has been interpreted as evidence for the poet's involvement in a 'religious/institutional'[13] group. While there are several religious fragments in the Sapphic collection, the main problem of reading these as confirmation of her involvement in an all-female group is the lack of consistent evidence as to who sang Sappho's songs and, more importantly, the context in which they were performed. On these issues, André Lardinois comments that it is possible that 'besides … more or less choral songs, there were genuine monodic songs, performed only by Sappho herself; after all the *Suda* speaks of Sappho's monodies as well as lyric songs'.[14] He further notes that the only occasion known to scholars where monodic songs were performed in the age of Sappho was the symposium (male banquet).[15] While we have little if any conclusive evidence for a female equivalent of the symposium in the Archaic era, scholars such as Lardinois and Marilyn B. Skinner suggest the possibility of such an environment.[16]

Sappho's poetry has been read from decidedly different perspectives as generations, indeed centuries, have passed, and some scholars now regard past emphasis on Sappho 'the schoolmistress' or Sappho 'the priestess' as not only outdated but homophobic. On the portraits of Sappho as the mature, spinster-like educator of young ladies, Holt N. Parker writes: 'This whole construction was created to explain away Sappho's passion for her "girls", allowing her the emotion of love but denying it any physical component.'[17] This debate over Sappho's status within the aristocratic community of Mytilene is indicative of the many ways in which she has captured the (predominantly) Western imagination for centuries. Naturally, the unease that often characterises the response of scholars is a consistent theme in the history of Sappho from the fifth century BC onwards.

Renaissance readers knew Sappho primarily from Ovid's fictional account of a letter by her to her male lover, Phaon, included in his collection of poetic epistles entitled *Heroides* (*The Heroines*). In *Heroides* 15, Ovid writes of Sappho's passion for a dashing ferryman by the name of Phaon, which leads her to reject her previous life as a lover of women. This poem, which sanitised Sappho's sexuality, was the inspiration for various writers and translators of Ovid determined to confirm the poet's heterosexuality for a Renaissance audience and beyond. Thus Alexander Pope (1688-1744), although not a trained Classicist, turned his hand to translating Ovid's epistle, and Robert Southey followed with *Sappho: A Monodrama* (1793). He in turn was succeeded by Mary Robinson in her 'Sonnets' (1796), several of which were based on Sappho and Phaon.

Despite the attempts to erase Sappho's predilection for women, which clearly emerges from what remains of her work, alternative receptions of her poetry and life are also present. John Donne (1572-1631) in his 'Sappho to Philaenis' challenges the heterosexual Sappho championed by his contemporaries and provides a celebratory exploration of female-female love, as illustrated in lines 44-50:

And betweene us all sweetnesse may be had;
    All, all that *Nature* yields, or Art can adde.

My two lips, eyes, thighs, differ from thy two,
　　But so, as thine from one another doe;
And, oh, no more; the likenesse being such,
　　Why should they not alike in all parts touch?
Hand to strange hand, lippe to lippe none denies;
　　Why should they brest to brest, or thighs to thighs?

Philaenis was a name well known in antiquity: she was the alleged author of an erotic manual produced in Greece some-time during the third century BC; the name was also used by the Latin epigrammatist, Martial (*c.* AD 40 – *c.* 104), to denote a particularly abhorrent female whose abnormal, masculine tendencies led to acts of depravity with both sexes. It is possible that Donne may have been familiar with Martial's poem (7.67), but, in view of its nature, it seems more likely his inspiration came from the reputation of the erotic writer.

While Sappho also became a source of inspiration for women writing verses on homoerotic desire – a tradition that continues to the present day – as early as the seven-teenth century comparisons with Sappho were made as a means of praising well-known and respected female poets. Thus, in the preface to a 1667 edition of the verse of Katherine Philips (1631-1664), Sir Charles Cotterell wrote: 'We might well have call'd her the English *Sappho*, she of all the female Poets of former ages.'[18] Cotterell, however, goes on to temper the comparison – 'As for her Vertues, they as much surpass'd those of *Sappho*' – to protect the reputation of Philips who, ironically, extolled the pleasures of intimate female friendship. In relation to Philip's work, one may suggest that her use of Sappho was subtle and intuitive, namely that she recognised in the Sapphic corpus a distinctly female and female-oriented voice that served as a poetic and, more importantly, hermeneutic model for the representation of her own sexual transgressions (as perceived by the society of the day).

In view of the historical preoccupation with Sappho's sexuality, it comes as no surprise that she also featured as a protagonist in *Les Chansons de Bilitis* (*The Songs of Bilitis*), literary soft-pornography produced in 1895 by Pierre Louÿs. This enterprising author had, in fact, created a literary hoax, pretending that the short prose musings that constituted *Les Chansons de Bilitis* were in fact translations of ancient Greek poems written by a contemporary of Sappho, unearthed in Egypt. Outraged by the publication, Ulrich von Wilamowitz-Moellendorf (1848-1931) subsequently assumed the mantle of Sappho's protector, publishing a series of works in which he championed the poet's high morals, her admirable qualities as a wife and mother and, of course, her respectable status as a schoolmistress.[19] Wilamowitz was influenced by his master-teacher, the German philologist Friedrich Gottlieb Welcker (1784-1868), whose work entitled *Sappho von einem herrschenden Vorurtheil befreyt* (*Sappho Freed from a Reigning Prejudice*) is, as the title suggests, a determined – even dogged – account of Sappho the morally pure (read 'heterosexual').

It seems fair to say that in view of Wilamowitz's passion for creating an idealised lifestyle for his Greek heroine, which was as much a fantasy as Louÿs' erotica, he would be devastated at the appropriation of Sappho by the female writers, feminists and lesbians who followed in his wake. From the passionate lyrics of Katherine Philips in the seventeenth century to Mary Robinson (1758-1800),

Virginia Woolf (1882-1941) and Adrienne Rich (1929-), Sappho has been a source of both poetic and personal inspiration.

1

Sappho's Lives

Various references to Sappho from the ancient world deal with her talent as a poet and are lavish in their praise. But there is also a derogatory tradition, one concerned with the nature of her sexuality and, to a lesser extent, her appearance. Bernadette J. Brooten comments on the former representation: 'During Sappho's own lifetime, we hear neither of disapproval of her erotic inclinations nor of debate about them, but in later centuries, wild speculation ruled the day.'[1]

The more prurient representations of Sappho come from scant fragments of Greek comedy from the late fifth to the fourth century BC. These remains do not mention Sappho's attraction to women, although we cannot assume such a theme was absent. Lardinois, however, is adamant that 'Sappho was never portrayed as a lesbian on the Athenian stage, but, quite to the contrary, as an extreme heterosexual'.[2] This may be in keeping with the comic stereotype of the women of Lesbos as licentious or, alternatively or concurrently, it may have been intended as irony. The fragments do support Lardinois' argument; for example, one from Diphilus (fourth century BC) states that the Ionian poets Archilochus (seventh century BC) and Hipponax (sixth century BC) were the lovers of Sappho. Similarly, Antiphanes (fourth century BC) in the *Leucadius* wrote of Sappho's passion for Phaon as did Menander (*c.* 341 – *c.* 293 BC) in the *Leucadia*, from which come the following lines:

Where Sappho first, so runs the tale,
    in wild love pursuit of proud Phaon
    leapt from a far-seen promontory,
harkening now to the vow we made
    grant praise, great king,
    of your shrine shall ring
    upon the cliff Leucadian.[3]

There is no textual evidence in what remains of Sappho's work that attests her love for Phaon, although she may have mentioned the ferryman's story in poems now lost, which in turn may have inspired the tradition. The legend appears in various testimonies of the poet's life from post-antiquity, as illustrated in this entry from the tenth century AD work, the *Suda* (*Fortress* or *Stronghold*):

Sappho, a Lesbian from Mytilene, a lyre-player. This one leapt from the cliff of Leucates, drowning herself, out of love for Phaon the Mytilenaean. Some have said that she also wrote lyric poetry.[4]

The most extensive treatment of Sappho as the lover of Phaon, and a likely source for the *Suda* account, is Ovid's *Heroides* Letter 15: Sappho to Phaon. The first fifteen poems that comprise the *Heroides* (possibly published in *c.* 15 BC) are elegiac compositions written by women to lovers or husbands. The letter from Sappho to Phaon was once regarded as spurious, although most recent scholarship now accepts it as genuinely Ovidian.

In view of his opinion of same-sex relations, Ovid appears to be enthusiastic about saving Sappho's reputation through his revival of the Greek comedic tradition, as shown in lines 17-20:

Anactoria is of little worth to me, of little worth is shining
    Cydro,
      not pleasing to my eyes, as before, is Atthis,
and the hundred other girls whom I loved without reproach;
      worthless man [Phaon], you alone have what once
    belonged to many girls.[5]

Ovid has Sappho renege on her previous sexual tendencies,
claiming that her love for Phaon has ended her attraction to
women. Ovid also casts Sappho as she sometimes casts herself
– namely as the suffering elegiac lover – the lover rejected or
abandoned by the beloved. As Ovid's tragic heroine, Sappho,
thwarted by Phaon, writes in the concluding lines of the
letter (217-20) that the only option left for her is suicide – to
jump from the Leucadian Rock:

If it is pleasing to have fled far from Pelasgian Sappho –
    though you will find no good reason to run from me –
at least let it be spoken of to miserable me in a cruel letter,
    in order that my fate be sought in the Leucadian water.

Phaon is a mythical character. The ancient stories depict him
as an old ferryman who willingly transported the goddess
Aphrodite in his craft without requesting payment; in return,
the goddess transformed him into a beautiful youth.
Germaine Greer, writing on the ancient mystery of Sappho's
love for this mythical figure, states:

Phaon is clearly not a historic personage but a personification
of absolute and irresistible beauty, in much the same way as
Adonis. The inclusion of Sappho amongst the victims of his

beauty would seem to indicate that the poet too had become to some extent mythologised.[6]

Ancient and post-ancient authors, poets and artists did, most certainly, mythologise Sappho. The tradition of her passionate desire for Phaon prevailed throughout the Renaissance and beyond, particularly in translations and rewritings of Ovid's poetic epistle, which had reappeared in Europe around the beginning of the fifteenth century.

English versions of *Heroides* 15 at times over-played Sappho's rejection of her former female lovers, thereby re-inforcing her heterosexual change of heart, inspired by the ferryman. In the English version by Wye Saltonstall of 1636, for example, lines 17-20 of Ovid's poem (quoted above) read:

> I hate Amythone, and Cyndus white,
> And Atthis is not pleasant in my sight.
> And many others there were lov'd of me,
> But now I have plac'd all my love on thee [Phaon].[7]

Saltonstall's expurgated rendition, written for 'the Vertuous Ladies and Gentlewomen of England', was much more genteel than the Latin text read by their husbands.

In addition to the Phaon love story, there also existed an alternative Sappho biography, one that did, in fact, emphasise her attraction to her own sex, and one that was at times judgemental of her private life. The *Suda* also records the life of this 'other' Sappho:

> Sappho, daughter of Simon or Eumenus or Eerigyius or Ecrytus or Camon or Etarchus or Scamandronymus; her

mother was Cleis. She was a Lesbian from Eresus, a lyric poet, she flourished in the 42nd Olympiad [612/608 BC], when Alcaeus, Stesichorus and Pittacus were alive. She had three brothers, Larichus, Charaxus and Eurygius. She was married to a very wealthy man called Cercylas, who traded from Andros, and she had a daughter by him called Cleis. She had three companions and friends, Atthis, Telesippa and Megara, and she received ill-repute from her disgraceful friendships with them. Her pupils were Anagora of Miletus, Gongyla of Colophon and Eunica of Salamis. She wrote nine books of lyric poetry, and she invented the plectrum. She also wrote epigrams, elegiacs, iambics and solo songs.[8]

This account, while essentially objective, appears to include information of a spurious nature that has been taken at face value. In addition to the identity of Sappho's father, which is obviously uncertain (although other sources mention a Scamandronymus), the name of Sappho's husband, 'Cercylas', is more than likely a dirty pun derived from the Greek comic tradition, as it can mean 'Penis' or, less decorously, 'Prick'. This, combined with her husband's alleged trading base, Andros, renders the phrase 'Cercylas ... from Andros, as 'Prick ... from the Isle of Man', as 'Andros' is connected etymologically with the Greek noun *aner* (man).[9]

In view of the pun, it would seem unwise to take any of the information seriously. Nevertheless, Sappho's fragments do contain references to Cleis:

I have a beautiful child who looks like golden
flowers, my precious Cleis, for whom I would not
take all of Lydia, or delightful (Lesbos) ... (*fr.* 132)

But for you Cleis, I
cannot obtain a decorated
headband ... (*fr.* 98[b])

Brief as these fragments are, they are informative, particularly if we assume that the poetic voice is a personal one and that Sappho is speaking about herself and her child.[10] Read accordingly, the first fragment extols a mother's love and is a celebration of the gift of a daughter, while the second one is part of a longer verse that describes Sappho's views on the beauty of young women adorned with glorious headbands. These fragments, almost poems in miniature, inspired several versions such as the one by John Herman Merivale, written in 1833:

I have a child, a lovely one,
In beauty like the golden sun,
Or like sweet flowers of earliest bloom;
And Claïs is her name, for whom
I Lydia's treasures, were they mine,
Would glad resign.

As for Sappho's brothers, she mentions at least one, most likely Charaxus (*fr.* 5.1-10):

Cypris and Nereids, permit my brother
to arrive to this place unharmed,
and that all he wishes for in his heart
be granted,
and permit also his atonement for all the mistakes
of the past and that he be a joy to his loved ones

and a blight on his enemies,
and that none again be a sorrow to us.

Permit him to willingly bring honour
to his sister ...

The nature of her brother's mistakes is unclear in this fragment, although another piece (*fr.* 15) suggests his involvement with a woman, Doricha, about whom Sappho seems most indignant. Charaxus' relationship with Doricha is also attested in later sources: the historian Herodotus (fifth century BC) and the geographer Strabo (*c.* 63 BC – *c.* AD 21).[11] Both writers state that Doricha (sometimes called Rhodopis) was a prostitute who was freed from slavery by Charaxus, with Herodotus adding that it was this liaison, no doubt an embarrassment to the aristocratic family, which led Sappho to censure her brother's behaviour.

As quoted above, the *Suda* also tackles the subject of Sappho's sexuality, noting that Sappho 'had three companions (*hetairai*) and friends (*philoi*), Atthis, Telesippa and Megara', and that her reputation suffered because of her 'disgraceful friendships (*aischrai philiai*) with them'. The latter adjective evokes images of shame, humiliation and disgrace, hence when applied to Sappho it describes behaviour considered to be depraved or base. In contrast, *hetairai* are companions,[12] while *philoi* are those who are loved, and can be used of close friends, family and spouses. Therefore, according to the *Suda*, it is not Sappho's intimate friendships that were frowned upon, but their sexual nature, which caused great shame.

Atthis is mentioned by Sappho in several fragments: 8, 49, 96 (the most complete piece) and 131; Megara is referred to only once (*fr.* 68[a]), while Telesippa's name does not appear at all. The relationship between Sappho and Atthis appears to have been very intense (see Chapter 4). Sappho writes of her love for Atthis, yet, as with her other lyrics about women, there remains not a single word, phrase or context that proves conclusively that the love assumed a sexual form. What remained of her work in antiquity, which we may assume was essentially a complete poetic corpus, may have been more explicit, but not necessarily so. While Sappho's environment may have enabled close companionship between women, and also clearly permitted education of aristocratic women to a high degree, it would have been too radical a challenge to the patriarchy for a female poet to publicly describe unambiguous, indeed explicit, physical love for other women.

The complexities of the constructions of sexuality in ancient societies are markedly different from those of the modern Western world, which makes any classification of Sappho and her love of women a challenging task for the modern interpreter. There is, however, a potentially informative description of these very issues in the *Orations* by Maximus of Tyre (*c.* AD 125-185):

> What alternative is there for one but to refer to the love of the Lesbian woman as the Socratic art of love? To me, they seem to have practised love in their own special way: she the love of women, he the love of men. Indeed, they claimed to have loved many, being captivated by all things beautiful. What Alcibiades and Charmides and Phaedrus were to him, Gyrinna and Atthis and Anactoria were to her. What the rival craftsman Prodicus and Gorgias and Thrasymachus and Protagoras were to Socrates, Gorgo and

Andromeda were to Sappho. Sometimes she criticised them, at other times she scrutinised them, employing irony like Socrates.[13]

Maximus is one of the few ancient commentators who attempted to analyse Sappho's sexuality from a more balanced, comparative perspective, associating her love of women with Socrates' love of young men. As the scholar clearly relies on his readership's familiarity with Platonic dialogues, which discuss Socrates the 'lover', he clearly sees little need to elaborate on his statements. Maximus would, therefore, assume that his readers understood the concept of Platonic Love as symbolised by Socrates in works such as the *Symposium*, Plato's dialogue on the meaning of *eros* (physical desire, erotic love, love per se), in which Socrates expounds upon the attainment of a higher love, a love that acknowledges physical attraction but strives to surpass it.

While Maximus' view is a sympathetic one, we do not possess enough of Sappho's work to establish clearly how closely her views on the love of women correspond to those of Socrates as represented by Plato. Maximus' observations may be interpreted, however, in a conceptual way, namely as an attempt to classify both Sappho and Socrates as lovers of their own sexes who sought to express that love in a non-sexual way. Such an interpretation of the passage from the *Orations* fits the Sapphic fragments, although there is at times an erotic edge to Sappho's work, just as there is in certain scenes from Plato's dialogues in which Socrates finds it difficult to ignore the physical charms of certain young men.

Maximus' references to Sappho's attitude towards the young women named also recall the debate concerning

Sappho the teacher, Sappho the leader of some female group on Lesbos. Admittedly, his reference is not as strong as that in the previously quoted *Suda*, which names her students, Anagora, Gongyla and Eunica – none of whom are mentioned in the fragments. As we have seen, however, Atthis does feature in Sappho's remaining work, as does Anactoria (*fr.* 16), as well as Gyrinna (*frr.* 29, 82[a], 90), but none of these women are referred to as students. The references to Gorgo (*frr.* 144, 213) and Andromeda (*frr.* 57, 68[a], 90, 131, 133[a]), while not exactly positive, are basically too fragmentary to furnish any definitive interpretation of Sappho's relationship with them.

The poetry

For a poet whose extant work comprises few complete poems, several semi-complete poems and approximately two hundred fragments – some consisting of a single word – the fascination with Sappho is excessive. Most of her work was lost some time in late antiquity and some of what remains today was discovered at Oxyrhynchus (modern-day el-Behnesa in Egypt) during excavations in the early twentieth century. The excavation site at Oxyrhynchus was originally a refuse dump and has yielded letters, public documents, legal and financial transactions as well as magic spells and pieces of famous literature by authors ranging from Homer to the Greek playwrights, Plato to Saint Paul.

Sappho's 'Hymn to Aphrodite' was preserved by the literary critic Dionysius of Halicarnassus (first century BC) in his treatise *On Literary Composition*. Herein, Dionysius quotes Sappho's verse in full as an example of smooth, perfectly structured style:

It tries to combine and interweave its component parts, and thereby produce, as far as possible, the effect of one continuous utterance. ... the style resembles finely woven stuffs, or pictures in which the lights melt insensibly into the shadows. It requires that all the words be melodious, smooth, soft as a maiden's face ...[14]

Other fragments have survived via a similar process. In the work entitled *On the Sublime* (first century AD), ascribed with some uncertainty to the Greek rhetorician Longinus, one of Sappho's most famous pieces, *fr.* 31, has been preserved as an example of a poet's ability to capture a series of complex and competing feelings:

Sappho ... always selects emotions associated with the madness of love from the attendant circumstances and the real experience. Where does she reveal her talent? In her adeptness at choosing and combining the most vital and extreme concomitants.[15]

Open to various interpretations, as discussed in Chapter 4, *fragment* 31 *may* be seen as the poet writing from personal experience and describing a passionate, virtually unbearable response to the sight of a desirable woman who sits beside a man – a man declared to be 'as fortunate as the gods'. Alternatively, scholars today tend to stress the non-personal or non-autobiographical nature of Sappho's songs, arguing instead for the primacy of her role as a lyric poet who dramatised situations for performance.

In view of the high reputation of Sappho's poetry during antiquity, it is surprising that her collections did not survive in anything resembling a complete or nearly complete form. This is the story for many authors, however, including some of the most revered names in the ancient Western canon. It seems that survival was often a matter of chance. Margaret Reynolds hypothesises that Sappho's poetry merely ceased to be popular: 'it seemed that scribes and their employers thought Sappho an arcane taste, not worth the labour of retranscription. Gradually all her Nine Books disappeared.'[16] Harriette Andreadis takes a different line of argument, suggesting that Sappho's work was systematically 'lost during the depredations of Christianity',[17] implying that their content, or composer's life, or composer's gender, or all three, were factors involved in the destruction. Indeed, there has been a scholarly tradition maintaining that Christians actually burned Sappho's books, but there is scant evidence for this. Additionally, there is the theory that since Byzantine references to Sappho seem to have disappeared after the twelfth century, the Crusaders could have been responsible for the destruction of her works, along with those of other ancient writers.[18] The fact is, however, that we simply do not know why her compositions virtually vanished.

Transformations of Sappho

The process of recovering the work of the Tenth Muse began in Italy and France in the sixteenth century. In Venice in 1508, Aldus Manutius included *poem* 1 in an edition of Dionysius of Halicarnassus, followed by the publication of *fragment* 31 in the 1554 edition of Longinus' *On the Sublime*. In France, Henri Estienne published the pieces preserved by Dionysius and Longinus in conjunction with the known fragments in a 1566 edition of Greek lyric poetry. English editions followed in the seventeenth century and Western readers once again began to appraise Sappho and her world independently of Ovid and Phaon. This is not to suggest that the seemingly indestructible legend of Phaon did not persist, rather that it and Ovid began to be slowly superseded by a return to the *poetry* of the *poet* herself.

With this revival came reinterpretations of the verse. Sappho's work and Sappho the woman both became sources of inspiration for male and female writers alike. So began the Sappho 'industry'. Raphael included her in his vision of Parnassus, the mural that adorns the Stanza della Segnatura in the Vatican; produced in 1511-12, the work featured only one mortal woman – Sappho. Less sublime was John Lyly's *Sappho and Phao* (*c.* 1582), a play written for Queen Elizabeth I, and intended as a clever, though not so subtle, compliment to the monarch. Lyly's virginal Sappho was a noble and learned ruler who held court at Syracuse. Although the ubiquitous Phaon makes an appearance (possibly a playful reference to the Duke d'Alençon who was busy wooing the queen at the time), Sappho (or is it Elizabeth?) rejects the passions of the body and thereby triumphs over love.

The Sapphos of Raphael and Lyly, both radically different and represented in two distinct artistic genres, the fresco and the farce, nevertheless reveal an important feature of what was to become the Sappho 'industry', namely the symbolic use of the poet to suit a specific context and message, be it personal, philosophical, political, and the list goes on. Joan DeJean states that 'Sappho is a figment of the modern imagination', adding that 'During her recovery by early modern scholars, she was completely a French fantasy.'[19] She was also, however, as DeJean herself admits, a fantasy, a figment of the imagination, long before she fell into the clutches of Renaissance scholars, artists and poets, be they French or otherwise.

DeJean's work on Sappho focuses on the reception of the poetry in France from the sixteenth to the twentieth centuries, and indeed there was once what Greer calls a 'Sappho craze'[20] there. In 1670 Jacques Du Four de La Crespelière produced the first French translation, although the one usually heralded as the first, most likely because it aimed at a more scholarly readership, is the 1681 edition by Hellenist Anne Le Fèvre Dacier. Although an acclaimed intellectual, Dacier was not a woman ahead of her time. In fact she professed that tales of Sappho's love of women were disseminated by those envious of her talents.[21] Not surprisingly, Dacier lent her full support to the Phaon saga.

Baron Longepierre also lent his support to the Phaon affair in the biography included in his 1684 French edition. But, unlike the steadfast Dacier, he did acknowledge that there was also the 'stain' of Sappho's encounters with women, a 'stain' revealed in what remains of her poetry and one that cannot be 'cleansed'.[22] Such early French editions clearly reveal the anxiety surrounding same-sex desire (particularly) between females, an anxiety that was not so radically different from the ancient attitudes. Like the ancients, the Renaissance Europeans regarded such desire as decidedly unnatural and, in the Christian environment, an act against God.

Ironically, it was the father of Anne Le Fèvre Dacier, Tanneguy Le Fèvre, who was one of the few pre-twentieth-century editors to acknowledge Sappho as primarily a lover of her own sex. His 1664 edition of her work, which included a biography, reveals his uncompromising stance on the issue of her sexuality. DeJean best encapsulates Le Fèvre's courageous contribution to the study of Sappho:

> In the balance he strikes between biography and commentary, Le Fèvre adheres to standards that subsequent editors would have done well to respect: he makes Sappho's life subservient to her poetry, mentions only those biographical elements he considers relevant to his description of her odes, and concentrates on providing a conclusive demonstration of Sappho's extraordinary literary status in antiquity.[23]

Le Fèvre was, unfortunately, a rarity. The views of Sappho as either a lover of men, namely her husband, then Phaon, or as a lover of women and therefore a highly problematic if not embarrassing poet to negotiate, continued to sit side by side in a most uncomfortable biographic and poetic union until well into the twentieth century.

As new editions of Sappho's poetry continued throughout Europe and Britain, so did accounts of her life. Based largely on the existing fragments, Ovid's *Heroides* 15, the works of contemporary scholars and more than a dash of personal imagination, these biographies clearly reveal that whichever 'Sappho' one chose to write about, she was inevitably a personal one. One of the most damning of these creations is described by Domitius Calderinus (1447-1478), who included a biography to accompany his 1476 edition of Ovid's epistle:

> ... Ovid indicates that her poems were lascivious ... [She] did not fail to love [them] in the manner of a man, but was with other women a tribade, this is abusing ... them by

rubbing, for tribein ... is to rub ... and she was named by Horace *mascula Sappho* ...[24]

If scholars did not denounce Sappho's sexuality, they white-washed it with excessive and obsessive attention to the Phaon story, which may be interpreted as a more genteel approach to what was likely regarded as repellent behaviour.

Calderinus and his views stand in stark contrast to an earlier work by Giovanni Boccaccio (1313-1375). Entitled *De Claris Mulieribus* (*On Glorious Women*), Boccaccio's entry on Sappho is idealised, romantic and just as unreal and incomprehensible as Calderinus' vituperative picture of a depraved tribad:

> The poetess Sappho was a girl from the city of Mytilene in the island of Lesbos. No other fact has reached us about her origin. But if we examine her work, we will see part of what time has destroyed returned to her; that is, the fact that she was born of honourable and noble parents, for no vile soul could have desired to write poetry, nor could a plebeian one have written it as she did. Although it is not known when she flourished, she nevertheless had so fine a talent that in the flower of her youth and beauty she was not satisfied solely with writing in prose, but, spurred by the greater fervour of her soul and mind, with diligent study she ascended the steep slopes of Parnassus and on that high summit with happy daring joined the Muses ...[25]

Boccaccio goes on, and on, and for a scholar who opens a biography with an acknowledgement that little is known of his subject's life, he manages to present a rollicking tale. His apprehension concerning Sappho's female relationships is revealed by its absence – he remains silent about her girl-friends.

Sappho had an obvious appeal to women from her time until the present. This is also a constant theme in the twisted, tangled tales of her life. In *Le Livre de la Cité des Dames* (*The Book of the City of Ladies*) by Christine de Pisan, written in 1404, the sense that women sometimes regard Sappho as being known intimately to *them* is revealed:

> The wise Sappho, who was from the city of Mytilene ... This Sappho had a beautiful body and face and was agreeable and pleasant in appearance, conduct and speech. But the charm of her profound understanding surpassed all the other charms with which she was endowed, for she was expert and learned in several arts and sciences, and she was not only well-educated in the works and writings composed by others but also discovered many new things herself and wrote many books and poems.[26]

This reference to Sappho's beauty is at odds with the passage quoted in the Introduction that depicted the poet as 'contemptible' in appearance, 'exceedingly ugly', 'dark in complexion' and of 'considerably small stature'.[27] In the papyrus from which this description originates, the unknown author previously described Sappho's reputation thus: 'Some have accused her of being irregular in her ways and a lover of women.'[28] The connection between her sexuality and appearance is likely an example of the ancient tendency to link external qualities with inner ones – Sappho did not conform to the expected roles of a woman, thus she was regarded by many ancient authors as sexually 'abnormal', therefore she acquired a reputation for unattractiveness.

The tendency to conflate perceived immorality with ugliness is not found in the descriptions of Sappho in the works of Plato and Plutarch (first/second centuries AD), nor in Christian writers such as Eustathius (twelfth century AD), nor in the Byzantine author Anna Commena – all of whom describe her as beautiful. Interestingly, however, the unflattering physical portrait of Sappho remained in currency into the twentieth century. *Fragment* 52 (literally translated as: 'I do not hope to reach the sky with my two arms') is rendered thus by Classicist J.M. Edmonds: 'This little creature, four feet high, cannot hope to touch the sky.'[29] Readers should be grateful to Emily Dickinson's ' "Heaven" – Is What I Cannot Reach!':

'Heaven' – is what I cannot reach!
The Apple on the Tree –
Provided it do hopeless – hang –
That – 'Heaven' is – Me!

The Colour, on the Cruising Cloud –
The interdicted Land –
Behind the Hill – the House behind –
There – Paradise – is found!

Her teasing Purples – Afternoons –
The credulous – decoy –
Enamoured – of the Conjuror –
That spurned us – Yesterday![30]

There is clearly no one portrait of Sappho. We know almost nothing. But this has not stopped authors from antiquity to

the present day presenting their own, their confidently definitive or creatively imaginative 'Sappho'. She has become an
icon, a symbol for poetic genius; subversive love; celebratory
female-female passion; insane, obsessive heterosexual ardour;
women's emancipation; women's liberation; lesbian liberation.
What the creators of Sappho's biographies rarely consider
amid their tales of burning desire, self-destructive behaviour
and literary genius is the actual environment in which the
poet lived and composed. The world of Archaic Mytilene is
almost always overlooked – until recently.

The Archaic world

In 'Sappho's Public World', Parker begins with a quotation
from the fifth-century BC comic playwright, Aristophanes:
'War will be the concern of women', taken from the satirical
play, *Lysistrata* (*l.* 538). Parker's point in citing the line is to
open a topic for debate, namely that Sappho existed – like the
women of *Lysistrata* – in an environment that was subject to
war and, like them, may well have held strong political views.
Parker's point of emphasis is to challenge the long-held image
of Sappho as a poet who drifted through fields of flowers,
weaving wreaths for her golden-haired girlfriends and
pouring the occasional sweet-smelling offerings to Aphrodite,
goddess of bodily delights.
According to Parker:

> Every age creates its own Sappho. At the moment our own
> dominant image of Sappho is a private, and often explicitly
> Romantic/romantic one. Sappho is a locus where, oddly
> enough, the prejudices of the past and the projection of the
> present become bedfellows.[31]

As the images and representations discussed so far have revealed, Parker's point about 'creating' 'Sappho' is pertinent. Obsession with biographical manufacture has indeed meant that there has been little attention paid to what was happening in the public world of sixth-century Lesbos.

On the Parian Marble, a Greek chronological table found on the island of Paros, the following information is recorded:

> From the period when Sappho sailed into exile from Mytilene to Sicily ... the earlier Critias was archon at Athens, and in Syracuse the Landholders held political dominance.[32]

This inscription suggests political turmoil in Mytilene during the Archaic era and the effect this had on Sappho, who appears to have been in exile sometime between 604 and 595 BC. In the concluding lines of *fragment* 98(b), Sappho refers to Cleanax (possibly the tyrant Myrsilus, who ruled Mytilene during her exile) and to *phuge* (banishment). The political situation seems to have been most unstable, with tyrants (non-legitimate leaders) rising and falling from power, and intense factionalism among aristocratic families.[33] Sappho's poetic contemporary, Alcaeus (born *c.* 620 BC), also from Mytilene and also exiled (for opposition to Myrsilus and his ally, Pittacus), makes several references to the unstable environment, which appears to have reinforced the idea among scholars that Sappho was, by comparison, apolitical. This does not mean, however, that she was indifferent to the public world, nor that her surviving works are devoid of such commentary.

Sappho attacks members of rival aristocratic families, as is seen in a fragment directed at a certain Mica, whom she calls 'evil one', who allegedly 'chose the friendship of women of the house of Penthilus' (*fr.* 71). The 'house of Penthilus' refers to the former ruling clan of Mytilene, also mentioned by Alcaeus,[34] renowned for its brutality and oppression, and into which Pittacus, tyrant of Mytilene after the death of Myrsilus, married. There are other such references, and if read from a political perspective, they may provide evidence for a different Sappho to the one we are accustomed to reading about. Such an approach to her work – one that lays aside the obsession with the private world of the poet – is also useful in shedding new light on some of the names included in the fragments. In the previously cited passage from Maximus' *Orations*, for example, Gorgo and Andromeda are named as the rivals of Sappho. The enmity between Sappho and these two women has been traditionally interpreted as one based on poetic rivalry or romantic competition for the girls of Lesbos. Yet it is more likely that the women belonged to an opposing faction, the clan of the Polyanactids (Offspring of the Great Lord), and that Sappho is practising political vituperation.

Similarly, Sappho's censure of her brother, Charaxus, as previously discussed, rather than being the outpourings of an irritated sister, more likely indicates her awareness of the importance of maintaining a high familial reputation as befitted an aristocratic clan. Sappho was very aware of aristocratic feuding, factionalism and the imperative to maintain ancestral standing of the highest order. In this sense she was a product of her time, a time of political disorder in which she, as a member of a leading family, was an opinionated if not an active participant.

Sappho's partisanship – what scant evidence remains of it – has only recently occupied scholars. Despite its relevance to establishing a more accurate picture of the life of the poet, and indeed of the world of Lesbos in the sixth century BC, it will perhaps never supplant the dominant image of Sappho the lover. From Ovid's ubiquitous epistle, rendered in various editions for various readerships, the skewed biographies of the *Suda*, and the attempt at a more understanding approach to her life in the writings of Maximus, down to the French revival, Sappho is portrayed as a hopeless romantic, a passionate deviant, a brilliant poet, a paragon of female chastity. Such fabrications often pay little heed to the evidence in her poetry – poetry that speaks volumes despite its fragile state.

2

Songs for the Gods

Seated on your multi-coloured throne, Aphrodite, deathless,
guile-weaving child of Zeus, I beseech you,
do not with satiety or pain conquer
my heart, august one,   4

but come to me here, if ever at other times as well,
hearing my words from far away,
having left your father's house,
golden you came   8

having yoked your chariot. Beautiful swift
birds directed you over the black earth,
frequently beating their wings, down from the sky
then through mid-air   12

and quickly they arrived. You, blessed one,
smiling with your deathless face,
asked what I had suffered this time, why
I was calling yet again   16

and what I wished most to happen to me
in my mad heart. 'Who is it this time that I am to
persuade to take you back into her heart? Who,
Sappho, wrongs you?   20

And if she flees now, she will soon be chasing [you].
If she does not accept presents, she will give them.
If she does not love [you] now, soon she will,
even if she is not willing.'   24

Come to me now, also, and release me from harsh
care. All the things that my heart
desires for me – fulfil. You yourself, be my
ally in this enterprise.[1]   28

For over two millennia, this was the only complete poem preserved from the nine books of Sappho's verse. It has been the stimulus for numerous artistic imitations and scholarly interpretations. It is a hymn. It is a spell. It is egocentric. It is also, as shown by the quotation from Dionysius in Chapter 1, an outstanding piece of erotic verse.

This poem and *fragment* 2 that follows it have been the primary sources for those who have argued that Sappho was a leader – or at the very least, a participant – in a cult of Aphrodite. If she was not a teacher, Sappho was, for some, a priestess. This is unknowable. It is also unimportant when compared to what the poem reveals about Sappho's image of Aphrodite and her approach to homoerotic, albeit literary, courtship.

Aphrodite is usually defined as the goddess of love, but nothing seems further from the truth. To the ancient Greeks, Aphrodite was the embodiment of eroticism and passion, and if the term 'love' can be applied to her sphere, it is a love that is dangerous, out of control, potentially disruptive and not necessarily endorsed by the community. She may be invoked in marriage celebrations, particularly in her role as the giver of fertility, but she was just as readily available to assist adulterers as lovers of the same sex. While her history is shrouded in obscurity and academic disagreement, a common theory is that she was of Indo-European origin.[2] Although she was worshipped by Mycenaean settlers in Cyprus from as early as the twelfth century BC, her name is absent from Linear B[3] tablets from Mycenaean regions. In support of the Indo-European interpretation, however, it should be noted that Linear B is so fragmentary that the absence of her name may be simply a matter of chance. Additionally, the significant links between her and goddesses such as the Mesopotamian Ishtar and the Phoenician Astarte may be more indicative of inter-cultural contacts than Aphrodite's Near Eastern origins.

Literary accounts of the origins of the goddess are also contradictory. Homer (*c.* eighth century BC) claims she was the child of Zeus, the pre-eminent deity, and Dione, one of the Titans,[4] an explanation typical of ancient Greek accounts of divine ancestries, with Zeus, the master of all spheres, celestial and human, fathering deities by immortals and mortals alike. In contrast, Homer's contemporary, Hesiod, provides an alternative account of Aphrodite's birth, claiming that she came from the severed genitalia of a sky-god, Uranus.[5] In Hesiod's version, preserved in the aetiological poem, *Theogony*, Aphrodite arises from the foam of the mutilated member, which had been tossed into the sea by Uranus' treacherous son, Cronus, and arrives at Cythera, an island off the south coast of Laconia and the goddess's principal site of worship. Sandro Botticelli's *Birth of Venus* (*c.* 1480) is a glorified and romantic vision of this ghastly story.

Such divergent stories of the gods and their origins were commonplace among ancient authors, and the selection of specific details was largely a matter of choice for the individual author. Thus, Sappho's Aphrodite represents what she personally envisions as *her* goddess, and the portrait that emerges is one of an ally in erotic matters, a fighter on behalf of the poet in a lover's battle. Yet Aphrodite is also an unpredictable collaborator, for she has the power to torture Sappho with the pangs of unfulfilled desire. As a fickle divinity – as were her fellow Olympians – she could as easily act *against* the poet as in her favour.

Poem 1 clearly depicts Sappho's attraction to a female, although we know nothing about the object of desire except that she has rejected the poet. Aphrodite's role is to assist Sappho in claiming the recalcitrant female,[6] hence the reverential opening of the poem, in which the goddess is properly evoked with several standard epithets: 'deathless', 'guile-weaving', 'child of Zeus' and 'august one'. Noticeable also is the intimate approach to Aphrodite, which is effortlessly included alongside the more formal tone of supplication. Sappho evokes a close relationship between herself and Aphrodite, even going so far as to include the recorded words of the goddess. The fantasy of it all is cleverly conveyed, as the poet creates a poetic hymn in which the deity herself appears, intervenes in Sappho's dilemma and speaks. There is also a trace of self-deprecating humour in the poet's image of herself as a familiar suppliant in need of regular counselling in matters of the heart.

Sappho's Aphrodite is the child of Zeus, not the Hesiodic goddess born from the foam, but a deity closer to the more personal one who features in Homer's *Iliad*. She is also 'guile-weaving', which is not meant to be an insult, but rather an acknowledgement of the goddess's abilities to contrive innovative – even deceptive – ruses to ensnare an object of desire. The Greek word, *doloploke*, combines the concept of contrivance with the activity of weaving, hence 'guile-weaving', and thereby denotes a particularly feminine characteristic. Women in ancient Greece were, in fact, believed to be adept at guile *and* weaving. Homer's Penelope, the chaste wife of the hero of the *Odyssey*, was one woman who combined both talents. Penelope's devotion to her absent husband, Odysseus, led to the clever ruse whereby she informed her suitors that she would choose one of them the moment she had completed weaving a shroud for her father-in-law. But, unbeknown to them, the wily Penelope undid the weaving each night, thereby delaying the selection of a new husband. The weaving of guile in matters pertaining to sex and romance was, therefore, the preserve not only of clever heroines such as Penelope, but also of the goddesses who oversaw and even orchestrated such business.

As a 'guile-weaving' goddess, Aphrodite appropriately smiles, an image evocative of the secrets and snares she possesses. Such a representation is symptomatic of Sappho's familiarity with the epics of Homer. In the *Iliad*, the goddess's epithet, 'sweetly smiling', is ascribed to her some six times. Indeed Sappho's extant work, most notably *fragment* 31 (discussed in Chapter 4), reveals a significant debt to the author(s) of the *Iliad* and the *Odyssey*[7] and is further evidence of her superb education as well as her artistic ability to transform established literary material based on her own, unique interpretations.

The gods as portrayed by ancient poets and bards are in stark contrast to most modern, Western sensibilities. Both Homer and Sappho represent deities in keeping with the Greek concept of them, namely as anthropomorphic beings who are, essentially, exaggerated versions of humans. The gods, particularly the twelve Olympians, are more beautiful, more emotionally excessive and more powerful than the humans over whom they have significant control. They are worshipped in public festivals and in household rituals, yet simultaneously feature in mythological narratives and literature, appearing as characters as 'real' or dynamic as any mortal. Hence, Sappho casts Aphrodite as a companion, a mentor and supporter in her love life as well as a poetic persona who speaks to her.

As Sappho's poetry is early in the Greek canon, it is difficult to discern whether her portrait of Aphrodite is in keeping with established imagery from religious or cult iconography. Her 'multi-coloured throne' is possibly an allusion to the representations of deities in the Homeric epics,[8] although such depictions are also found on pottery from at least the time of Sappho. Both sources suggest that she was 'thinking of the Olympian goddess seated at home in heaven, not of any particular cult-divinity with cult-statue in a shrine on earth'.[9] The image of Aphrodite's personal chariot pulled by birds is not attested in literature or art prior to Sappho's poem. Scholars have offered various interpretations of the scene, some theories being based on the translation 'sparrow' for the Greek *strouthos*, which consequently leads to discussion of the bird's reputation for wantonness and fertility in ancient bestiary lore – thus making it an appropriate animal totem for this goddess. Such an interpretation is well attested in ancient sources, but Sappho predates these, thereby rendering the construal problematic. Perhaps the image belongs to a pre-literate belief still current in Sappho's time that the gods invisibly descended to earth preceded by a divine sign, in this instance Aphrodite's avian entourage, which served as a signal of their imminent presence.

The depiction of Aphrodite arriving in a chariot is suggestive of the means by which Sappho builds on Homeric themes, specifically the association between love and war. Underlying the *Iliad* are the dual themes of love and war, expressed in the story of Menelaus' heroic quest to retrieve his wife Helen from her abductor-lover Paris. Although the war is primarily motivated by Menelaus' need to regain his reputation rather than his wife, Homer's juxtaposition of the two seemingly discordant themes establishes a trope that inspires generations of ancient writers of erotic verse. Aphrodite's key role in the cause of the Trojan War, discussed in detail below, further accentuates the trope.[10]

Sappho stands at the beginning of the poetic tradition that exaggerates, dramatises and inverts the tension between the Homeric theme of love and war and love *as* war. Accordingly, the image of Aphrodite arriving in her chariot drawn by birds is suggestive of her role as an awesome participant in the battle of attraction and desire, possibly the commander-in-chief. Sappho, who presents herself as sharing an intimate relationship with the goddess, depicts her as an esteemed fellow-fighter, an ally, in her crusade to win over or subdue a certain female. In addition to calling on a divine co-fighter, the poet virtually portrays the nameless female as an challenger over whom she is determined to triumph. Having briefed the commander of the situation, Sappho is assured that the fleeing opponent will inevitably submit: 'she will soon be chasing you', she soon will be offering gifts, she will soon love 'even if she is not willing' (*ll.* 21-4).

Such an analysis of the poem, which emphasises Sappho's aggressive stance in matters pertaining to desire, is somewhat at odds with some scholarly readings, particularly those from a feminist perspective. In the latter, the emphasis is often on the equality between lover and beloved, in contrast to the traditional power dynamics involved in male-male relationships. In ancient Greece, most notably the Classical era,[11] it was customary for adult male citizens predominantly from the upper classes to court young men from the same social circles. In keeping with the traditions and ethics involved in such courtships, the adult (*erastes*) assumed the active or dominant role whereas the youth (*eromenos*), usually aged between thirteen and seventeen, assumed the passive role.[12] These distinct and disparate roles are regularly evidenced in male-authored texts and the visual arts, sometimes to an excessive degree whereby the youth is reduced to a powerless object of desire.

It is true, as most feminist scholars observe, that Sappho's poetry does not generally overstate a power imbalance between the lover and the beloved. Thus Skinner writes: 'In contrast to the male *erastês*' adversarial relationships with his love object and with the god afflicting him, her dealings with both mortals and divinities seem mutually rewarding.'[13] Nevertheless, Sappho's hymn to Aphrodite does reflect an important male sensibility, namely the dual theme of power and powerlessness. Detectable in the promise of the goddess (*ll.* 21-4), it is this attitude towards the beloved that Sappho seems to regard as the desired outcome. The psychology here is clever and somewhat dissembling, for by placing what may only be regarded as her own wishes in the words of Aphrodite, the poet distances herself from revealing what it is she truly seeks, namely the submission of the woman in question. By using the military image of Aphrodite the charioteer, as well as the martial vocabulary, Sappho augments – perhaps inadvertently – the male approach to passion. Love is war.

Love is also pain. As Sappho conveys her fantasies about conquering her woman, she also reveals that she herself fears being conquered, as evidenced in lines 3-4. While bringing exquisite sexual joys, Aphrodite also brings pain, the agony of unrequited love. This is a common motif in ancient litera-ture: thus Apollo is the god of both healing and disease, alleviating ailments and causing them. His twin sister, Artemis, goddess of the young and also of childbirth, is called upon to ensure safe deliveries and also carefully propitiated in case she harms mother and child.

Powerful sexual drives and their attendant emotions were viewed with anxiety in antiquity, and in this respect Sappho is no exception. This apprehension is also something Sappho shares with the patriarchy, for from the age of Homer's *Iliad* through to the authors of the Roman Imperial era,[14] the largely male-authored texts speak of the dangers of love, the dangers of the 'gifts' of Aphrodite and Eros (the personifica-tion of love, particularly mindless desire). Sappho displays her concerns not only in this hymn but elsewhere, as revealed in the following fragment (*fr.* 130):

> Eros the loosener-of-limbs once again shakes me,
> that sweetly-bitter, utterly irresistible little beast.

Despite the fragment's brevity, it contains similar if not the same sentiments as the hymn. As she reveals in her plea to Aphrodite, Sappho acknowledges in this piece that she is aware of the consequences of falling in love, or, perhaps more accurately, falling in lust, yet she understands that it is an 'irre-sistible' force – an 'irresistible little beast', and she will once again submit to the pleasure and the pain. In such poetic admissions, the reader becomes conversant with Sappho's self-awareness: *herpeton* designates a beast or animal that moves on all four legs – a creature that creeps – and it seems that no better word can describe the silent entity that is passionate craving. Sappho, in her choice of noun, further suggests that she is fully aware that this *herpeton*, which can also means 'snake' or 'reptile', is more than capable of a nasty bite.

In contrast to *poem* 1, *fragment* 2, her second major extant piece on Aphrodite, is more formal and ritualistic in content and tone. Preserved on a pottery shard, the fragment was found in Egypt and is now displayed in Florence at the Biblioteca Laurenziana, 'cradled in velvet like a holy relic'.[15] The material on which the text was inscribed, often referred to as *ostrakon*, was not a common means of recording literature, as *ostraka* were usually employed for more utilitarian purposes such as tickets for entry to public amenities, receipts for payments and school exercises (so, perhaps, an ancient school master copied this verse for the benefit of his pupils). Whatever the context in which it was inscribed, the piece represents one of the earliest surviving recordings of Sapphic verse, having been dated between the third and second centuries BC.

The fragment describes a sacred grove of Aphrodite and the poet addresses the deity, summoning her to earth (as she does in *poem* 1) to an altar at which a ritual is about to take place:

To this place, to me, from Crete to this temple
holy, where your charming grove
of apple trees is, and altars smoking
with incense;   4

and here cool water murmurs through apple branches
and the whole place with roses
is shadowed, and from quivering leaves
deep sleep flows down;   8

and here a horse-pasturing meadow blooms
with spring flowers, and the winds
breathe gently ...
...   12

There you, Cypris, having taken ...
delicately in gold cups
nectar mingled with festivities,
pour.   16

In establishing a scene that befits the goddess, Sappho presents a series of images that play on the senses. As Jack Winkler observes: 'Virtually every word suggests a sensuous ecstasy in the service of Kyprian Aphrodite (apples, roses, quivering followed by repose, meadow for grazing, spring flowers, honey, nectar flowing).'[16] In its utopian landscape, this almost mythically perfect scene encapsulates icons appropriate to Aphrodite; the roses and apples for example, redolent with sensuality, are standard motifs associated with her literary portrayals. In an early representation of the goddess, she is depicted thus (*Cypria, fr.* 6.1-7):

[Aphrodite] adorned herself with garments fashioned by
the Graces and the Seasons, [garments] dipped in the spring
        flowers
worn by the Seasons: crocus, hyacinth,
bountiful violet and the beautiful bloom of the rose,
sweet and succulent, and in ambrosial buds,
flowers of narcissus and lily. These perfumed garments
Aphrodite wears at all seasons.[17]

The passage continues with a description of Aphrodite, her companions, the Nymphs and Graces weaving floral crowns as they sing sweetly 'on the mount of multi-fountained Ida' (*fr.* 6.12). Such a pastoral scene, by a poet of the Homeric age, may just as well have been composed by Sappho and perhaps is indicative once again of her familiarity with established epic literature.

Elsewhere Sappho utilises the powerful symbolism inherent in flowers and fruit to depict images of feminine sexuality, as evidenced in her marriage hymns. Sappho also uses the symbolism in connection with Cleis (*frr.* 98[b] and 132), as noted in Chapter 1. In these fragments, the beauty, innocence and sensuality of young women are evoked through floral imagery, with flowers evoking the delicacy, fragrance and overall beauty of female skin.[18] As the goddess of irresistible attraction, corporeal delights and beauty – indeed feminine beauty – Aphrodite is, appropriately, the deity most regularly associated with such symbolism. As a goddess of fertility, she is also suitably connected with flowers.

As the goddess's shrine is fertile with roses, spring meadows and spring flowers, it is also shaded by apple trees. The apple as a symbol of the goddess most likely has its mythical origins in the story of the cause of the Trojan War. At the celebration of the marriage of Peleus and Thetis, the goddess Eris (Strife) tosses an apple on which is inscribed 'for the fairest', and immediately begins a squabble between Aphrodite and her fellow goddesses, Hera and Athena, and a beauty competition ensues. A hapless mortal, Paris, is chosen by Zeus as the judge and, through bribery – Aphrodite promises to give Paris the most beautiful thing in the world, namely Helen – the conniving goddess is awarded the apple.

In both Greek and Roman mythical belief, the apple was a token of love and to 'say that a person had been "struck by an apple" was tantamount to saying that he had been "love-struck" '.[19] It was also, not surprisingly, a symbol of fecundity when Sappho employed the apple as a comparison to a virgin in a marriage hymn (*fr.* 105[a]). Sappho's acknowledgement of Aphrodite's symbolic connection with the fruit is gently playful in her placement of an actual grove of apple trees within one of the goddess's earthly precincts. Aphrodite's sacred site bears the very fruit used in the games of love instigated by the divinity herself.

Scholars have long debated whether or not *fragment* 2 was actually intended to be performed at a religious ritual or festival. The fact that the language is, as Winkler notes, 'both religious *and* erotic',[20] adds to the vagaries inherent in a debate that extends beyond *fragment* 2 to encapsulate the entire remains of the Sapphic oeuvre and the context in which the poems were presented or performed.

Hephaestion's *Handbook on Metre* (second century AD) cites an extract from another of Sappho's poems (*fr.* 140[a]):

'He is dying, O Cytherea, gentle Adonis; what are we to do?'
'Beat your breasts, maidens, and tear at your garments.'

As with *poem* 1, there is a dialogue, here between a group of young women and the goddess. In *fragment* 140(a), the maidens have replaced the voice of the poet, but Aphrodite remains the respondent. Such examples, in addition to what we know of the oral nature of Archaic Greek poetry, point to the likelihood that many of Sappho's lyrics were performed in a public context. Accordingly, in relation to this fragment, we may assume there was a chorus of females and a single singer, perhaps in the role of the chorus leader, who assumed the role of the goddess, the context for the performance probably being of a religious or cultic nature.

As scholarship on Sappho's lyrics developed during the last decades of the twentieth century, there has been a greater emphasis on the poet as a composer of choral odes rather than monodies. Judith Hallett, for example, has argued that 'many of Sappho's fragments thought to be personal, autobiographical statements might in fact be part of public, if not marriage, hymns sung by other females'.[21] Such opinions have contributed to new ways of analysing Sappho's verse where the emphasis is on the cultural specificities of Archaic Greece rather than on the voice of the personal poet known to us from early modern times.

Fragment 2 certainly suits the argument that there were verses intended for choral performance at public occasions; the wedding hymns discussed in Chapter 5 were also, almost certainly, intended for recital at actual ceremonies. Other fragments of a religious nature further the interpretation of the public temperament of some if not many of Sappho's lyrics. *Fragment* 17, a hymn to Hera, may be interpreted along such lines:

Near to me (while I pray, be your gracious form,
revealed), O queenly Hera,
to whom the Atreidae, (renowned)
kings, made prayer(?);   4

after having accomplished (many labours),
first around (Ilium, then on sea),
they travelled towards this island,
but could not complete the voyage,   8

until (they summoned) you and Zeus,
'God of Suppliants', and Thyone's lovely (child);
now (be gracious and assist me) according to that
ancient tradition.   12

Holy and beautiful ...   13
maiden(s) ...   14
to be ...   15
...

...

...
to reach ...   19
(the shrine) ...   20

In accordance with a reading that accepts the choral, public
nature of *fragment* 17, the poem could be an invocation to
Hera, performed during a festival in her honour, a hymn to
the goddess to assist worshippers in their journey to a
shrine, or a plea for her to avert some undisclosed potential
hazard (possibly danger at sea). The reference to 'maidens'
(*parthenoi*) at line 14 may be to a female choir, but as it
belongs to an extremely fragmented section of the text, it is
unwise to be definitive concerning the identity of the
parthenoi: are they, for example, young women or
goddesses? That there appears to have been a temple on
Lesbos dedicated to the three gods mentioned in Sappho's
hymn nevertheless furthers the interpretation of the cultic,
and therefore public, nature of the fragment. Alcaeus, who
also composed a hymn to the divine trio, refers to this
temple (*fr.* 129.1-9):

… the Lesbians
… dedicated this vast conspicuous precinct
for all to share, and in it erected altars
of the holy gods: 4

they named Zeus 'God of Suppliants'
and you, the Aeolian, 'Glorious Goddess,
Mother of All' and this third one
they name 'Kemelios',   8

the eater of raw flesh.

Alcaeus, like Sappho, refers to Zeus with the epithet *antiaon* (God of Suppliants) and the god Dionysus is designated by the epithet *kemelios*, the meaning of which is unknown. The title *omestes* (Eater of Raw Flesh) refers to the ingestion of uncooked, unprepared meat in Dionysian ritual. In contrast, Sappho prefers the epithet for Dionysus denoting maternity, 'Thyone's lovely (child)'. While Sappho specifically names Hera, Alcaeus again uses an epithet, 'Glorious Goddess, Mother of All', which has been interpreted by scholars as a reference to the goddess, although this reading is not definitive.[22]

Sappho's hymn presents Hera in a specifically localised context. She rewrites a tale known to her from the Trojan cycle, recorded in Homer's *Odyssey* (3.130ff.), which tells of the departure of the Greeks from Troy. Half of the army remained at Troy with Agamemnon, while the others left under the leadership of Menelaus, Odysseus and Nestor. Nestor and his men sailed to Lesbos, later followed by Menelaus' crew, where they remained until they received a sign from Zeus as to the safest route home.

In Sappho's version, details are altered. She places both brothers, Menelaus *and* Agamemnon ('the Atreidae' mentioned in line 3; that is, the sons of Atreus) at Lesbos; additionally, the brothers do not pray to Zeus alone, but to what we may assume to be the trio of gods unique to cult worship at Lesbos: Hera, Zeus and Dionysus. The practice of establishing geographically, culturally specific interpretations of the gods, and thereby distinctive forms of worship, is a significant feature of Greek religion. In the case of Lesbos, this appears to have manifested itself in the combined precinct of the three deities.

There is no conclusive argument to explain the inclusion of Dionysus[23] in this trio; in contrast, Zeus and Hera, as siblings and also spouses, are regularly combined in all parts of the ancient Greek world. Dionysus, a later addition to the pantheon of Olympians, was the offspring of Zeus and Thyone (usually referred to as Semele, a mortal, daughter of the king of Thebes, Cadmus). Perhaps the addition is connected with the myth of Orpheus in which the magical poet and bard, once a follower of Dionysus, earned the god's wrath and was dismembered by his female followers, the Maenads. According to the story, his head (still singing) floated down the Hebrus, reaching Lesbos where it was buried.

Sappho sings to other Olympian gods as well as to the Muses (*poem* 58; *frr.* 44A[b]; 103; 124; 127; 128; 150; 187), goddesses of artistic inspiration and creativity. Again her interest is primarily in female deities. At times she adopts an intimate approach to the goddesses, most strongly evident in *poem* 1, which may well have been sung by Sappho herself, perhaps in a non-public context for a group of females. Other verses, such as *fragments* 2 and 17, are not as private in tone, and lend themselves to a more public, religious occasion. Aphrodite undoubtedly has a particular appeal to the poet. *Fragment* 5 recalls the cletic nature of *poem* 1, that is, the prayer format utilised by Archaic poets to express personal requests. In *fragment* 15, Sappho extends her prayer to include an apparently vindictive request of Aphrodite, namely that Doricha find the goddess 'very harsh' (*l.* 9).

Feminist scholars have contributed much to the advancement of studies on Sappho and her songs, although they may sometimes be too quick to assign an explicitly female voice to her lyrics.[24] When compared to the works of male contemporaries, Sappho's songs can, at times, appear quite similar, particularly her hymns. While *poem* 1 does seem to stand alone as a unique work of (female) authorship, the following hymn is indicative of a more traditional, public celebration of a goddess (here Artemis) not out of context in the patriarchal environment of Archaic Lesbos (*fr.* 44A[a]):

… (golden-haired
Phoebus), born of the daughter of Coeus,
having lain with the son of Cronus, (he of the lofty clouds),
great of name; but Artemis swore the (gods') powerful oath:
('By your head), I will remain a virgin,   5
(hunting) on the summit of (isolated) mountains.
Come and grant this now for my sake.'
She spoke thus, and the father of the blessed gods nodded
     approval.
(The Virgin, Shooter of Deer) she is called by gods (and
     mortals)
and Huntress, a great honour.   10
Eros, (loosener of limbs),
… approaches her not.

This fragment, published in 1952 by Edgar Lobel and Denys Page,[25] is from a papyrus roll dated to the second or third century AD. The assignment of the poet, however, was a problem, and remains so today. The two editors tentatively suggested Alcaeus over Sappho, their main argument being a metrical technique characteristic of his style. This metrical style is not, however, based on *fragment* 44A(a) but on the badly damaged second column of the papyrus that has been interpreted as the work of the same poet.[26] Understandably, Lobel and Page remained cautious. Page later attributed the ascription to Alcaeus on the basis of thematic content, stating: 'There is no evidence that Sappho wrote poems of this general type, whereas Alcaeus did so.'[27]

In contrast to this view, G.M. Kirkwood[28] argues in favour of Sappho as the author and highlights the very thematic content that Page denies *is* present in her verses. Page's reference to 'poems of this general type' is to those with an epic or, more precisely, a Homeric theme and (as noted in this chapter) there is a clear debt to the Archaic epic tradition in the poetry of Sappho. She may subvert this tradition at times but nevertheless she also writes in the style of the Homeric poets. A good example is *fragment* 44, which deals with the Trojan prince, Hector, and his wife-to-be, Andromache, both major characters in the *Iliad*. Kirkwood assigns *fragment* 44A(a) to Sappho based on his categorisation of both pieces as 'lyric narrative' that follow 'the standard "Homeric" story'.[29]

As stated above, *fragment* 44A(a) is not contrary to the patriarchal milieu of Archaic Lesbos. This is not out of kilter with a feminist approach to Sappho's poetry that argues for a gender-specific reading of her work. Indeed there is a distinctly female voice in many of her lyrics, but not all of them, and it seems a reasonable interpretation to posit that it is in her *epithalamia* or marriage-songs and erotic monodies that a female-centric intonation is most vividly expressed.

3

Mythical Lyrics

Sappho's verses clearly reflect a familiarity with the *Iliad* and the *Odyssey*. She imitates the themes, imagery and even the phraseology of these epics, which is a standard feature of the lyric poets of her time, but she also manipulates and alters the tradition most poignantly in her personal lyrics. She therefore acknowledges a literary debt to the Homeric poets while consciously deviating from them to produce individualistic works imbued with the erudite authority of the foundation masterpieces.

Chapter 2 noted the Sapphic version of the story of Hector and Andromache in *fragment* 44. This is arguably the most conventional of the lyrics dealing with Homeric themes. Sappho, for example, does not associate the pair with her own intimate world as she does in her erotic monodies (namely *fragment* 16 and *fragment* 23, discussed below), but retains an objective tone reminiscent of the Homeric poets. The choice of metre also captures the quality of the epic hexameter; although she chooses the glyconic metre, there is a dactylic extension that echoes the dactylic hexameter of the Homeric works. As Jane McIntosh Snyder comments: 'the hearers of the song would most likely have been expecting something relating to epic'.[1] Furthermore, there is the inclusion of 'Homeric phraseology',[2] the most recognisable being *helikopida* (glancing-eyed girl) to describe Andromache at line 6.

Preserved in one of the *Oxyrhynchus Papyri*, *fragment* 44 is – with the exception of *poem* 1 and the newly discovered *poem* 58 – the longest extant piece from the Sapphic collection:

Cyprus ...
... the herald arrived ...
Idaeus ... swift messenger
...   4
and the rest of Asia ... undying glory.
'Hector and his comrades are escorting a glancing-eyed girl
from sacred Thebe and the waters of Placia,
graceful Andromache, in ships over the briny   8
sea. Many golden bracelets and purple robes,
ornate delights, innumerable silver cups and ivory.'
He spoke thus. Quickly moved (his) beloved father, and the
message travelled to his companions throughout the
                spacious city.   12
Immediately the sons of Ilus yoked mules to
the smoothly-running carts, and a whole group
of women and (tender-)ankled virgins climbed aboard.
Separately (rode) the daughters of Priam ...   16
unmarried men led horses to the chariots ...
... and greatly
... charioteers
...   20
... like the gods ...
... holy ...
ventured out ... all together to Ilium,
the dulcet flute (and cithara) mingled   24
and the sound of the cymbals, and virgins
sang clearly a holy song,

and a divinely-sweet echo reached the sky ...
and everywhere along the streets was ...   28
wine bowls and cups ...
myrrh and cassia and frankincense mingled.
The old women cried out happily
and all the men released a delightful, high-pitched   32
song calling on Paean, the Far-Shooting, Skilled-in-the-Lyre,
and they sang in praise of godlike Hector and Andromache.

Admittedly, we do not possess any literature that describes the marriage ceremony of Hector and Andromache; nevertheless, *fragment* 44 continues the customary portrait of the pair as the archetypal husband and wife in the Homeric mythic tradition (especially in Book 6 of the *Iliad*). Although the piece is badly damaged in parts, it is possible to provide a relatively informative account of the scenario: the herald, Idaeus, announces the impending marriage to the people of Troy; Hector and Andromache are arriving by sea; the bride-to-be brings golden bracelets, purple robes and other precious items from her home at Thebe; the news stirs Hector's father, Priam (King of Troy), into action; the people of Troy begin preparations for the ceremony; the wedding hymns are sung, including a hymn to Apollo, 'the Far-shooting, Skilled-in-the-Lyre' (*l.* 33) and the customary praise of the couple seemingly concludes the piece (*l.* 34).

As mentioned above, this fragment lacks an overt personalisation of the themes of the Homeric epics, namely the insertion of the Sapphic or narratorial voice. Nevertheless, Page maintains that Sappho's skills as a re-interpreter are evident in her elaborate description of the marriage preparations. He further suggests that such picturesque detail may have been inspired by the wedding traditions of Mytilene: 'her portrait is not drawn from tradition or from imagination but from contemporary life.'[3] Specific details found in the fragment, but nowhere in the *Iliad* and *Odyssey*, are regarded as evidence of contemporary Mytilene as the source of inspiration:

> The σατίναι, carriages for women, might be seen in the streets, and the myrrh, cassia, and frankincense on the altars, of modern Mytilene: they have no place in Homeric Troy. The language is traditional; the story is her own design. The old and the new are fused and transmuted into a new element.[4]

Despite his thesis, Page (along with other scholars)[5] notes the brief, general depictions of marriage scenes in Homer's description of the Shield of Achilles (*Iliad* 18.491-6) and the short epic, *The Shield of Heracles* (*ll.* 273-84), sometimes ascribed to Hesiod.[6] Both scenes are worthy of consideration, for each contains specific narrative descriptions found in *fragment* 44, which in turn generate more or less the same tone of joviality inherent in the Sapphic piece. Both Homer and Hesiod, for example, specify the presence of youths and maidens as an integral component of the marriage celebration; there is an emphasis on bridal songs and musical accompaniment (pipes, lyres and flutes in the Hesiodic passage; flutes and lyres in the Homeric scene); Hesiod also mentions the use of carts for the transportation of brides-to-be, which is admittedly different from the Sapphic inclusion of vehicles for the transportation of the female wedding attendees. There is the inclusion in the earlier texts of bridal torches, a common feature in these nocturnal ceremonies, to which there is no reference in *fragment* 44, but little should be concluded from this omission owing to the poor state of the papyrus. Page further observes that she includes the mingling of 'myrrh and cassia and frankincense' (*l.* 30), which he regards as a culturally unique addition to Sappho's evocation of marriage.

In view of Page's interest in detecting what he regards as the unique qualities of the fragment, it is puzzling that he ignores Sappho's specification that females sang in the wedding choir. Indeed, the inclusion of the choir of maidens and also that of the old women is arguably the most significant point of departure in the piece. In the male texts, female participation is presented as something more passive in nature: Homer merely states that 'the women stood each before the door and marvelled' (*ll.* 495-6), while Hesiod, at least, includes maidens in the procession as torch-bearers and generally enjoying the festivities (*l.* 275-7). With Sappho's description of the 'virgins [who] sang a holy song' (*ll.* 25-6), the elderly women who 'cried out happily' (*l.* 31) and 'all the men [who] released a delightful, high-pitched song calling on Paean' (*ll.* 32-3), her emphasis is on the involvement of the whole community, as opposed to the Homeric and Hesiodic tendency to evoke a more male-oriented participation. Admittedly there is no reference to a choir of youths in *fragment* 44, but again this could be a result of textual fragmentation, especially in view of the reference to young men at lines 13-14, described as 'the sons of Ilus'.[7]

The subject of the fragment, its dactylic metre and its reference to Homeric characters, have led some scholars[8] to interpret it as one of Sappho's marriage hymns, composed specifically for performance at a wedding. This reading is impossible to refute, but it is also impossible to support with conviction. One could suggest that, in view of the fragments usually assigned to the category of Sappho's marriage hymns, *fragment* 44 appears to be of a different nature in its extensive treatment of Greek mythology[9] without allusion to an individual bridal couple or indeed to individual or social concerns relating to marriage as present in the *epithalamia*.

Whether the fragment belonged to a marriage hymn or not, by focusing on the preparations for the wedding ceremony, Sappho stresses the joyful, youthful love of the hero and heroine, in preference to the tale of the tragic destruction of this perfect union that features so poignantly in the *Iliad* (assuming that the fragment ends at line 34).

In contrast to the 'lyric narrative'[10] style that best describes *fragment* 44 and *fragment* 44A(a), Sappho reveals much more of a distinctive, original approach in her reworking of Homeric motifs in *fragment* 16 and *fragment* 23. In the former, one of her most famous songs, the poet weaves together a personal philosophy, a Homeric heroine, the theme of *eros* and the love of an absent friend, to create one of the most powerful and unique lyrics of the Archaic age:

Some believe a team of cavalry, others infantry,
and still others a fleet of ships, to be the most beautiful
thing on the dark earth, but I believe it is
whatever a person loves.   4

It is very easy to make this
clear to everyone: the one who by far
outshone all mankind in beauty,
Helen, abandoned her high-born husband   8

and sailed away to Troy with no thought whatever
for her child or beloved parents,
but led astray (by *eros* / *Cypris*?) ...
lightly ...   12

for (this)
reminded me
now of Anactoria, who is
no longer here;   16

I would prefer to gaze upon her
lovely walk and the glowing sparkle of her
face than all the chariots of the Lydians and their
armies.   20

In Sappho's exploration of the meaning of what defines 'the
most beautiful' she proclaims it is what a person loves,
stressing the importance of the individual as opposed to
the community. Hermann Fränkel writes of this revolu-
tionary affirmation: 'We do not desire what is in itself
beautiful, but we find what we desire beautiful. This anticipates half of the dictum of the sophist Protagoras,
according to which man is the measure of all things.'[11] The
example used to extend or explain this philosophy is the
story of the foremost heroine of the Homeric epics. Helen
abandoned her husband, Menelaus, and fled with her lover,
Paris Alexander, to Troy, and so began the Trojan War.
Sappho's interpretation of the relationship between the two
star-crossed lovers is apparently simple: Helen regarded
Paris as the most beautiful, and acted accordingly,
forsaking everything in pursuit of this ideal of 'the beautiful'. The example is, however, somewhat complicated,

Sappho

essentially because it is the beauty of *Paris* that motivates
Helen, although it is *she* who is regarded as the most beautiful of mortals (literally, in the Greek, 'the most beautiful
thing'). The inversion of the audience's expectation that
Paris should be the one striving to obtain 'the most beautiful thing' (Helen), as opposed to 'the most beautiful
thing' striving to obtain another, constitutes the chief
artistic conceit of *fragment* 16. The significance of this defiance of the anticipated metaphor reinforces Sappho's
premise: if Helen of Troy, in her personal choice of the
Trojan prince, Paris, demonstrates that what she, as an
individual, loves is the ultimate in beauty, then who is to
question the philosophy? In short, the personification of
beauty in the Greek world, Helen, defines beauty.

This is a radical departure from the Homeric tradition, yet
it is imperative to note that Sappho is composing in a
different genre. As a lyric poet, literally a composer of songs
for the lyre, Sappho is able to adapt her most influential
model to suit herself and also the contexts in which her songs
were performed; when she performs monody, or a solo song,
this freedom is even more readily available. Indeed, Sappho
can personalise and reinvent Homer in a way unacceptable to
the objective genre of epic. In a departure from the Homeric
epics and the predominantly masculine society they represent, for example, Sappho questions the idealisation of
cavalry, infantry and fleets. This is a rejection of the *Iliad* in
particular and its martial heroism. In preference to the this,
Sappho offers a definition of beauty based on what may be
described as a feminine prerogative.

The interpretations of feminist scholars (in particular) that
posit an explicitly female voice in Sappho's songs were
discussed in Chapter 2. There it was suggested that such a

reading does not apply to the hymn to Artemis. It does, however, pertain to a reading of *fragment* 16 with its re-visioning of the works and indeed the ethos of the Homeric poets. In addition to the ingenious redefinition of what constitutes beauty, Sappho imbues the narrator's lyric daydream or stream of consciousness with an intimate recollection of a beloved friend, Anactoria. It is Sappho's story about Helen's departure from Sparta, her child, her parents and 'her high-born husband' (*l.* 8), which inspires the memory of Anactoria. Herein we witness not only Sappho's mastery of the lyric genre with its potential to reinterpret established myths but also her particularly feminine rendering of traditionally masculine themes, as demonstrated below in the comparison between her treatment of the Helen myth and that of Alcaeus.

The specific details of Anactoria's gait and glowing skin, which dominate the narrator's mental images of the absent beloved, lend a unique tone of reality or authenticity and sentiment to the fragment. Though she is clearly beautiful, it is not merely the beauty of Anactoria that evokes the comparison with Helen (despite it being implicit) but rather the theme of abandonment. Helen leaves Sparta for Troy because she is led astray; the verb *paragein* is used in this context to suggest a non-rational force that interferes with one's mind.[12] Most editors insert '*eros*' (or *Cypris*) for the lacuna of line 11, which is in harmony with the metrics and is a suitable noun to accompany the verb. It may therefore be inferred that Anactoria also left because she was impelled by the forces of *eros*.

Sappho does not condemn Helen (or Anactoria) for her actions. Nor does she allude to the disastrous consequences of Helen's departure, namely the setting in train of the Trojan War to retrieve her. This non-moralistic approach to the story of Helen is unique among the coterie of Archaic lyric poets who, with the exception of Sappho, are male (insofar as the extant works stand).[13] The relevant fragments of Alcaeus, for example, are decidedly condemnatory:

Alcaeus *fragment* 42:

As the tale is told, owing to wicked deeds
caused by you, Helen, sorrowful grief came to
Priam and his sons, and Zeus with fire
destroyed sacred Ilium.   4

Not such was the gentle virgin
whom the noble son of Aeacus married,
taking her from Nereus' halls to Chiron's
home,   8

having invited all the holy gods to the wedding;
he untied the pure virgin's girdle,
and the love of Peleus and the best of Nereus'
daughters burgeoned;   12

and within a year she gave birth to a son,
the most excellent of the demigods, blessed
driver of chestnut horses. But they died for the sake
of Helen, the Phrygians and their city.   16

Alcaeus *fragment* 283:
...
...

... and (*eros / Cypris?*)
in her breast, thrilled the heart of the woman of Argos;

by the Trojan man, the breaker of hospitality,
she was driven mad, following the ship over the sea,   6

leaving her girl-child (forlorn) at home,
and the ornately-covered bed of her husband,
(since) her heart persuaded her (to submit) to *eros*,
(through the daughter of Dione) and Zeus;   10

...

... many of his brothers (the dark
earth) embraces, killed on the Trojan plain
for the sake of that woman,   14

and numerous chariots (broken) in the dirt,
and numerous black-eyed (fighters) were trampled,
and in the bloodshed, (rejoiced
... Achilles)   18

In the first fragment of Alcaeus, possibly a complete poem, he categorically blames Helen for causing the Trojan War. Here is a contrast with Sappho's *fragment* 16 that objectively explains that Helen was 'led astray (by *eros*?)'. In fact, Sappho is closer to the treatment of Helen in the *Iliad*, for there the poet implies that the Spartan Queen followed Paris not of her own accord, but under the influence of Aphrodite.[14]

Whereas Sappho simply mentions Helen because she pursued what she loved, Alcaeus' focus is on the horrendous results of the heroine's action. In his moral approach, 'almost unique in the Lesbians' according to Page,[15] Alcaeus contrasts Helen to Thetis (*ll.* 5ff.), describing the latter as 'the gentle virgin' (*l.* 5) and presenting her as the role model of the virtuous wife and mother. In regard to the well known tradition of the myth cycle involving Thetis, the sea-nymph, and her mortal husband Peleus, Alcaeus' simile is misleading as his audience would have been familiar with Thetis' early departure from the marriage and the raising of her son, Achilles. Additionally, through the evocation of the marriage of Peleus and Thetis (*ll.* 9ff.), Alcaeus foreshadows the infamous Judgement of Paris. Again, the poet's audience would have been familiar with the story of the goddess Eris who initiated the beauty contest between Athena, Hera and Aphrodite and the ensuing bribery of the latter, resulting in the Greeks' campaign to win back the glorious prize (Helen) awarded to Paris (discussed in Chapter 2). Through these images of marriage, birth (*ll.* 13ff.) and death (on the fields of Troy: *ll.* 15-16), Alcaeus emphasises the destructive consequences of Helen's beauty, the doer of 'wicked deeds' and bringer of 'sorrowful grief' (*ll.* 1-4).

In Alcaeus' second fragment, the sentiments expressed again reveal a lack of empathy when it comes to Helen, although the suggestion that she was influenced by the powers of *eros* (or perhaps even the god, *Eros*, the personification of erotic power) or *Cypris* (Aphrodite), make the version closer to Sappho's *fragment* 16. Additionally, Alcaeus' mention of Helen's madness (*ll.* 4-6) is further evidence for an interpretation that argues for the likelihood of either *eros* or the Cyprian goddess as the cause of her state of mind and subsequent actions. However, the emphasis in both fragments on the devastation wreaked as a result of Helen's elopement marks Alcaeus' decidedly oppositional interpretation of the myth compared to Sappho's treatment of the same material. Where Sappho focuses on individuals, namely Helen and Anactoria, Alcaeus is concerned with the wellbeing of a community; where Sappho shows little if any interest in the effects of Helen's abandonment of husband and child, Alcaeus articulates his criticism by strongly contrasting the elopement of Helen and Paris with the sanctioned union of Thetis and Peleus.[16] In these two divergent treatments, Sappho reflects on a private world, Alcaeus on a public one.

In *fragment* 23, recorded on a badly preserved piece of the *Oxyrhynchus Papyri*, Sappho sings of Helen once more:

> ... (hoped?) ... of *eros* ...
> ...
> (for when) I look at you face-to-face,
> (not even) Hermione (seems) like you,   4
> and to compare you to golden-haired Helen
> (is not unwise).
> ... for mortal women, yet know this,
> by your ... (you) would (liberate) me   8
> from all my cares. ...
> ... (river) banks ...
> ... all through the night ...
> ...   12

As with *fragment* 16, this piece clearly reveals Sappho's use of the heroine and her beauty to evoke the loveliness of a mortal woman. With less certainty, we may posit that the singer – as in *poem* 1 – is calling on a divine force, either *Eros* (*l.* 1) or Aphrodite, to intervene in some way, as lines 8-9 read, to '(liberate) me / from all my cares'. The reference to *eros* in line 1, further suggests that the singer, perhaps Sappho, is in the grip of passion – as Helen was in *fragment* 16 – which would explain a plea to one of the appropriate gods for relief. If such tentative readings are accepted, the object of desire may be detected in the form of a female whose beauty is comparable to that of Helen's only child, Hermione, and indeed to that of Helen herself.

Why Sappho was drawn to Helen as a poetic point of comparison is open to speculation, but one may hypothesise that Helen's ultimate beauty was the most flattering means to praise the loveliness of a mortal woman, a possible object of desire. Additionally, comparisons between mortals and the divine were not as common or, more precisely, not as elaborate in the lyric genre, compared to epic. In the former, mortals are usually associated with the gods in marriage songs and poems in honour of an individual's victory at a competition. In contrast, Homer, an epic author whose work precedes the lyricists and whose narratives involve semidivine heroines and heroes, is under no such restraints of religious etiquette.

The following quotation from the *Iliad*, in which the Trojan Elders gaze upon Helen and compare her to the goddesses, would have been well known to Sappho (*Iliad* 3.154-60):

When, therefore, they saw Helen going to the tower,
they softly spoke winged words to each other:
'Is it not a cause for anger that the Trojans and well-greaved
Achaeans should suffer woes for a long time over such a
      woman?
She is terribly like immortal goddesses in face.
But even so, though she is like that, let her go home in the
      ships,
and let no trouble be left for us and our children hereafter.'

74

The words of the old men present a case for an under-standing of Helen's predicament, namely that she cannot be blamed for causing the war, nor can the men who fight for her be censured, for her beauty is so extraordinary – so divine – that it inspires forces in humans beyond her control. In short: Helen is powerless to control the forces of *eros*, the forces of chaos, which her beauty compels. Daniel H. Garrison comments: 'Although Helen blames herself for the evil effects of her sexuality, Homer is at pains to imply that the gift is not her fault. It is the nature of any *aretê* or pre-eminence that it is a divine gift over which the recipient has no control.'[17]

Once someone gazes on another so beautiful, one regarded by the observer as 'the most beautiful thing' (*fr.* 16.2-3), it is virtually impossible to resist following one's heart. As Helen is the embodiment of this maxim, her appeal to Sappho is understandable. Not only did Helen inspire the forces of *eros*, she was also the victim of them. Sappho makes this explicit in *fragment* 16 through the use of the verb *paragein* (*l.* 11) and the likely possibilities of the accompanying noun. Alcaeus recognised the difference between the mad love of Helen and Paris, contrasting it with the legitimate union of Thetis and Peleus. Similarly, when one views Sappho's treat-ment of the Spartan Queen, particularly in *fragment* 16, and in the light of her song on Andromache and Hector (*fr.* 44), one may posit that she too identified the passion of Helen and Paris as outside the parameters of acceptability.

Allusions to Helen and her story may be found elsewhere in the Sapphic corpus. To return to *poem* 1, for example, we find a singer, identified as Sappho, calling on the goddess to inflame the heart of an unnamed woman. In short, Sappho requests that Aphrodite exert control over the object of desire and *make* her fall in love. Sappho's comprehension of the powers of the goddess was also known to the Homeric poet. In Book 3 of the *Iliad*, for example, Aphrodite orders Helen to go to the bedchamber of Paris and make love with him. Helen, despite her protestations (*Iliad* 3.399ff.), eventually obeys the goddess, who has become exasperated at her attempt at defiance (*Iliad* 3.414-17):

'Headstrong girl, do not defy me, lest in anger I abandon you,
and despise you as much as I now terribly love you,
and lest I devise strong hatred between
the Trojans and the Danaans alike –
then you would die wretchedly.'

Like the Iliadic Helen, Sappho has an intimate relationship with Aphrodite. Nevertheless, while Sappho can pray to Aphrodite and successfully summon her, there is no suggestion in *poem* 1 or any of the surviving fragments that the poet was any less vulnerable to her divine will than Helen.

4

Love of Women

To the ancients, Sappho was a Lesbian but not a lesbian. While it is common to assume that the word 'lesbian', denoting a lover of women, derived from Sappho's place of origin, Lesbos, the etymological and cultural background is not quite so straightforward. The Greeks certainly provided us with the word, but it came from the verb *lesbiazein*, which literally means 'to behave as one from Lesbos', that is, 'to fellate'.[1] What the verb connotes is an act of unambiguous heterosexuality, and the historical explanation for the origin and meaning of *lesbiazein* appears to have been based on the reputation of the women of Lesbos for unbridled sensuality and lust.[2] In fact, the word 'lesbian' as it is understood by contemporary Western society has a short history, as Hallett explains:

> According to standard reference works, the English adjective 'Lesbian' denoted intensely erotic, hetero- more than homo-erotic, individuals and feelings until only a few decades ago. But its medical and 'underground' meaning, first attested in 1890, has gradually taken over as the existence of female homosexual liaisons has become more widely acknowledged among the educated, Anglo-American public.[3]

These comments rightly emphasise the cultural distinctions between the ancient and the modern usages of the word.

Hallett not only clarifies the short history of the term to designate 'female homosexual liaisons', but also indicates the differences between ancient and modern receptions of these relations.

It is important to note that in the Classical age and beyond, the periods that provide the most plentiful information on sexuality, female homoeroticism was an unacceptable activity; it was not regarded or respected as a lifestyle or personal choice, but as a taboo. In contrast, Greek males of citizen status were free to engage in relations with other males so long as specific societal traditions were maintained and no public shame was incurred by an individual or his family. Marriage was no impediment. As discussed in Chapter 2, adult Greek males could engage in erotic relations with youths; the latter were to assume the passive role in the relationship, both socially and sexually, while the adult assumed the active role. In keeping with public morals, it was shameful for these roles to be reversed or for the relationship to continue after the youth's assumption of manhood. Sources from the same period reveal that there was no such provision for similar relationships to be developed between women, with the exception of the women of Sparta.[4]

What we know of sexual mores in Archaic Greece is relatively scant in comparison to the well-attested eras of Classical and Hellenistic Greece. Nevertheless, in relation to male-male love, there is a poetic tradition (as illustrated below [p. 100] in the excerpt from Ibycus, which is probably homoerotic in context). In the Theognidean corpus (*c.* 540s BC),[5] for example, there is the strong motif of the desire for young men, which indicates that the parameters of *eromenos* and *erastes* had been socially established by the sixth century BC. In terms of female-female desire, there is little that remains of a definitive nature except for the lyrics of Sappho and the *Partheneion* (*Maiden Songs*) of Alcman (seventh century BC).[6]

That Sappho 'loved' her female friends can be verified by her surviving work. Likewise, the very existence of her fragments suggests a social tolerance of intense female relations in Lesbos during her lifetime, which is notably in contrast to the reception of such in later periods. Whether this love was sexually expressed remains unknown; it is certainly not specified in her extant work, with the possible exception of the last line of *fragment* 94 (discussed below). Nevertheless, participation in sexual intimacy is not mandatory for one's sexual identity, and while Sappho does not sing of 'making love', she does sing of sensual experiences. Anne Pippin Burnett describes it accordingly: 'One caress was as sweet as another, a wreath could be as provocative as an uncovered limb.'[7]

Post-Archaic biographies and literary caricatures aside, what is it that reveals Sappho's 'lesbianism'? In keeping with the ancient precept that defined sexuality in terms of an action, Sappho's vigorous engagement in a female-centred environment and her poetic evocation of an active desire constitute the essence of her sexuality – namely, what modern people call 'lesbianism'. Burnett's explanation of Sapphic love therefore provides a subtle insight into what may be defined as Sappho's erotic romanticism – for women. We cannot, however, confidently claim a specific 'lesbian' identity for Sappho according to definitions of the modern West. It is the poetry that must be read carefully in order to access the nature of Sapphic desire – pieces such as *fragment* 31, her most famous expression of female-female passion.

Here the poet speaks of a longing, unfulfilled and unresolved, which has become an emblematic statement for female lovers of women (*fr.* 31.1-16):

He seems to me equal in good fortune to the gods,
whatever man, who sits on the opposite side to you
and listens nearby to your
sweet replies   4

and desire-inducing laugh: indeed that
gets my heart pounding in my breast.
For just gazing at you for a second, it is impossible
for me even to talk;   8

my tongue is broken, all at once a soft
flame has stolen beneath my flesh,
my eyes see nothing at all,
my ears ring,   12

sweat pours down me, a tremor
shakes me, I am more greenish than
grass, and I believe I am at
the very point of death.   16

The hyperbole characteristic of many of Sappho's other songs, such as *poem* 1 and *fragment* 94, is given its most dramatic rendering in this piece. Sappho evokes a situation, sparsely described but nevertheless meticulously vivid, of a scene involving a man and two women. The man, unnamed and referred to merely with pronouns, sits and engages with a woman. This woman, also unnamed and designated merely with pronouns, talks and laughs and clearly beguiles both the man whose attention she commands – and who in turn commands her focus – as well as the female narrator who is virtually unable to control her reactions to the sight and sounds of such a creature.

The use of the demonstrative pronoun *kenos* ('that man there', or, as translated above, 'whatever man'), may be a ploy to emphasise the singer's attempt at disinterest and possibly disdain: Sappho or the Sapphic persona does not want to give him too much space within the confines of the lyrics. The comparison between the man and the gods is not meant as a compliment in the traditional sense, namely as a tribute to good looks or noble countenance, but acknowledges his good fortune in being seated next to such a wonderful woman and his seemingly super-human ability to contain himself while in her presence. The latter is evoked with similar economy: the sight of her (suggested in line 2 through the placement of the man across from her, indicative of his clear vision) and, more significantly, the sound of her, are all we have. It is the response of the third-party to the woman that reveals her outstanding beauty, her dulcet tones and her overall presence. In this choice of representation, Sappho again reveals her debt to the Homeric poets, who regularly evoke an image – of beauty or sheer horror – through the description of an observer's reaction to the sight. Accordingly, we recall, among other examples, the words of the Trojan Elders in response to Helen at *Iliad* 3.154-60, discussed in the previous chapter.

The brilliance of the poem results in part from the grandiose and highly charged drama of the narrator's responses. Sappho – or, reading the piece less subjectively – the poetic raconteur, is aflame with a series of powerful psychosomatic symptoms that place her, in her deluded opinion, on the brink of death. From line 6 to the end of the fragment, these symptoms dominate the piece to the exclusion of all else – the lines redolent with the Sapphic technique of inverted Homeric imagery, especially the re-workings of Iliadic depictions of wounded heroes.[8] Again, therefore, we recall the theme of love – or *eros* – as a battle or a war. Sappho, as she appears in *poem* 1, is once again a fighter, but here she appears to be defeated before the siege has begun.

Nothing from antiquity comes close to this piece for the representation of the debilitating effects of *eros* on one's physical, mental and emotional faculties. Through the concentration on her bodily symptoms, the singer expresses the simultaneous loss of her other senses, namely mind and spirit. Female-female desire – or any desire – in its rawness and most visceral manifestation is nowhere better conveyed. Not surprisingly, therefore, *fragment* 31 has inspired poets throughout the centuries. The Latin poet, Catullus (*c.* 84 – *c.* 54 BC), whose admiration of Sappho's lyrics is evident in several of his verses, was inspired to compose a version (*poem* 51):

That man seems to me to be equal to a god,
that man, if it is safe to say, seems to surpass the gods,
he who, sitting opposite you, again and again
    watches and hears you   4

sweetly laughing, which snatches all the
senses from wretched me. For as soon as I gaze at you
Lesbia, there is nothing more for me.
    …   8

But the tongue is numb, a subtle flame
spreads down through the limbs, with their own din
the ears ring, the eyes are covered with
    double night.   12
Idleness, Catullus, is bad for you.
In idleness you exult and participate too much.

Idleness, once before, has destroyed kings and
     prosperous cities.[9]   16

Catullus' *poem* 51 is close to the Sapphic original despite some major departures.[10] The metre is in Sapphic stanzas and Catullus experiences some, not all, of Sappho's ailments. He also personalises his version to a greater extent than Sappho does: he includes his name in the final stanza and also the name of his beloved (*l.* 7), the woman he calls Lesbia. The latter pseudonym is most likely in honour of his Sapphic muse and/or as a compliment to his mistress as a woman as beautiful as the women of Lesbos were renowned to be,[11] and as appreciative of poetry as they were.

Whereas Catullus' version of *fragment* 31 is an exercise in poetic skill and homage to both Sappho and Lesbia, the context of the original has been the subject of debate. Wilamowitz, whose work on Sappho was briefly discussed in the Introduction, argued that the fragment was an *epithalamium* and that the singer's duty, as was customary in marriage songs, was to praise the bride.[12] Therefore, he interprets the fragment as a traditional eulogy to the bride, the girl in the poem, and a subsequent compliment to the groom, the man who sits next to her, by a singer commissioned to write and perform at the ceremony. This interpretation, popular during the first half of the twentieth century, was expanded to incorporate the theory concerning Sappho the schoolmistress, also promoted by Wilamowitz, as we have seen, by explaining that Sappho's role was something more than a marriage chorister, but in fact she sang the song at the wedding of a favourite student.

There is little conclusive evidence to support this reading, and it is most likely a further example of Wilamowitz's determination to remove any traces of Sappho's sexual desires towards women. Nevertheless, the thesis was adopted and developed by other scholars, most vigorously by Bruno Snell in an article published in 1931.[13] In studies of Sappho's fragment from, mainly, the 1980s onwards, the general consensus favours a homoerotic interpretation.[14]

An analysis of some of the major constituents of the debate concerning the contrary readings of *fragment* 31 can be summarised accordingly: (1) comparisons between bridal couples and the gods are regularly detected in *epithalamia*, as noted in Chapter 3, but not exclusively; (2) on the latter debate, Page rightly observes that Sappho's phrase '*phainetai moi*' ('seems to me'), does not introduce a direct comparison between the man and the gods, as is often the case in wedding songs, but establishes a more personal observation; (3) further, Page states that such phrases are 'found in praises of men on any sort of appropriate occasion';[15] (4) the fragment does not expressly reveal depictions of a marriage ceremony. As George L. Koniaris states: 'in what we possess of the poem there is no use of the nomenclature of marriage ... no mention of parents, relatives, friends, no wishes for children, for a happy life, etc.';[16] (5) neither the recorder of the fragment, Longinus, nor the Latin poet who revised it, Catullus, respond in any way that suggests they read the piece as anything more than 'a masterpiece among poems of passionate love'.[17]

Sappho sings of another unnamed woman in *fragment* 94. As with the theme of the pain of desire so effectively dramatised in her other lyrics that address her passions for women, particularly *poem* 1 and *fragment* 31, this piece is about separation:

4. Love of Women

...

She, leaving me, wept   2

many tears, and spoke thus to me:
'What a terrible thing we suffer
Sappho. Truly against my will do I leave you.'   5

This is my reply:
'Be happy – go – and remember me,
for you know how much I cared for you.   8

But if not, I wish
to remind you
... and we shared beautiful things: 11

many wreaths of violets
and roses and ...
you put on, beside me,   14

and many garlands
woven from flowers
you placed round your delicate neck,   17

and with much costly perfume,
fit for a queen,
you anointed yourself,   20

and on restful beds
gentle ...
you would satisfy ... desire.'   23

Fragment 94 is also the subject of considerable debate, with
the main point of contention being the identity of the

speaker of the first extant line. The metrical structure indicates that the opening line is missing; therefore scholars must decide whether the speaker is Sappho (referred to by name in line 5, and who delivers lines 7-23) or the departing woman (who is given lines 4-5). The arguments for each specific reading are based in part on grammatical and metrical issues as well as on the tone and comparisons with other pieces within the Sapphic oeuvre. In regard to the latter two concerns, the first extant line does recall other hyperbolic outbursts, including the drama of *fragment* 31 and the intensity of *poem* 1 (in which the singer includes her own name in the words of Aphrodite), and would, therefore, not be out of character in regard to Sappho's own representation of herself as a poetic persona (assuming she sings of her own predicament – real or imagined – in *fragment* 31). On the contrary, the opening words resemble the tone of sheer distress observed in the lines clearly attributed to the unnamed woman in lines 4-5; in contrast, the words Sappho actually delivers in lines 7-23 may be melancholy, but are decidedly more controlled and comforting in comparison.[18] Ellen Greene contributes an additional comment on the differing emotional states of the speakers, reinforced in part by their differing temporal references: 'The woman sees the relationship only in light of the immediate reality of separation and loss, while the speaker sees it from the perspective of her interior world of memory.'[19]

There is intense passion in *fragment* 94 – expressed by both speakers. The unnamed woman's love for Sappho is so profound that she expresses a wish for death at the thought of leaving her. In contrast, Sappho urges her to 'rejoice' (*l.* 7), for while there is physical separation, there are beautiful memories of past experiences. The evocation of the sight, touch and smell of flowers and perfume creates an otherworldly atmosphere and draws one's attention to the sensuality of the female body: garlands are placed round a 'delicate neck' (*l.* 17) and costly unguent anoints flesh (*ll.* 18-20).

Sappho continues to reminisce but unfortunately the text becomes fragmented (*ll.* 22ff.). The restoration of lines 22-3 is problematic and scholars are yet to reach agreement. Lobel initially suggested '*nea*]*nidôn*' (literally, 'of young women') for line 23, which would give the following: 'you would satisfy the longing of young women.'[20] Lobel (and Page) subsequently rejected this reading and concluded that 'The matter must be left unresolved.'[21]

Fragment 96 was recorded on the same parchment as *fragment* 94; on the evidence of the handwriting once again, the manuscript has been dated to about the sixth or seventh century AD, and was first published in 1902.[22] Like *fragment* 94, it focuses on similar themes and is structured in the same three-line stanzas (*fr.* 96.2-17):

... often her thoughts turning this way   2

... (she honoured) you like
a goddess, conspicuous,
and she rejoiced in your song.   5

Now among Lydian women she stands out
as, the sun
having set, the rosy-fingered moon   8

surpasses all the stars; and her light spreads over
the salty sea
and flowery fields equally alike;   11

the dew is shed beautifully,
roses and delicate
chervil and flowery cow-parsley bloom.   14

Often going to and fro
remembering gentle Atthis with desire
her tender heart is eaten by reason of your fate.   17

The song, a consolation to Atthis, deals with the latter's mourning for an absent companion. It opens with a reminder to Atthis of the happiness she once gave this woman, she who honoured Atthis as a goddess and revelled in her song (*ll.* 2-5). This is followed by some of the most formidable lines composed by Sappho; the extended simile that is meant to comfort Atthis through the elaborate praise of her companion (*ll.* 6-14). This detailed evocation of nature not only creates, as it does in *fragment* 94, a faraway and exotic world, but also energises the text with powerful, yet subtle eroticism.

The woman, who has departed to Lydia, is compared to the moon; so outstanding is her beauty that she outshines all the Lydian women, just as the moon surpasses all the stars. While admiring the sheer beauty of these lines, scholars have sometimes dismissed the relevancy of the simile as it progresses, arguing that it has little to do with the subject at hand.[23] The perceived problems of the lines have subsequently led to various hypotheses as to their meaning and possible relevance. One common interpretation is that the image of the moon and the night symbolises the passing of time, as Rebecca Hague summarises: 'The most prevalent interpretation of the simile sees in the imaginary moon and night the real moon and the real night which the parted lovers pass in longing for each other.'[24] As Hague notes, however, this interpretation, like many others, is not based on textual evidence.

Scholars have also been concerned about the applicability of the extension of the image at lines 9ff. Here Sappho's depiction of the moon's light that spreads over the sea and over fields of flowers culminates in a picture of dew being shed on roses, chervil and cow-parsley.[25] The glow of the moon, however, is not an inappropriate image, emphasising as it does, quite naturally, the shining beauty of the woman. The moon per se has also been, historically, an archetypal symbol for women because of its monthly course.

Likewise, the connection between the moon and dew is found in Greek mythology: the goddess Herse or Erse is the offspring of the Moon (Selene) and Zeus.[26] Alcman describes the goddess of the dew thus (*fr.* 57):

Such things as are nurtured by Erse, daughter of
Zeus and Selene.

While the fragmentary nature of this text does not allow us to identify the 'things' nurtured by Erse, we may assume that Alcman, like Sappho, refers to plant-life. Additionally, Alcman's text makes an explicit mythological connection between the goddesses Moon and Dew, which may be interpreted as a thematic equivalent to Sappho's metaphorical connection. The connection between Moon and Dew as goddesses of fertility may well be, therefore, one of the major implications of the extended simile of lines 9ff. The moon brings forth the dew, just as Selene gives birth to Erse, and thus through the forces of nature or their divine personifications, the earth is nurtured and flowers bloom. The emphasis on the beauty of the moon and the fertility she encapsulates in connection with the dew combine to produce an intensely feminine image, or series of images, described by G.O. Hutchinson as 'the heaping rhetoric so characteristic of Sappho'.[27]

The *Suda* names Atthis as one of Sappho's 'companions and friends', one of the women with whom she engaged in a relationship, the nature of which earned her 'ill-repute'.[28] Before this account of the life of Sappho, Ovid had also referred to Atthis as one of Sappho's former lovers, one of the women eventually rejected as a result of her consuming passion for Phaon.[29] One wonders, in view of these two references to Atthis, whether Sappho wrote other poems of a more explicit nature on her erotic love for this woman.

Indeed, there are other references to Atthis, albeit scant, in the fragments of the Sapphic collection. In addition to *fragment* 96, there is a scrap of papyrus (*fr.* 8) that can be reconstructed to read simply:

… Atthis, to you …

There is also a quotation from Hephaestion (*fr.* 131):

… Atthis, the thought of me has become hateful to you, and you flee to Andromeda.

What is fascinating and perhaps illuminating about *fragment* 131, in addition to the strong impression that there has been a serious breakdown in the relationship between Sappho and Atthis (reading the work as biographical or otherwise), is the textual transmission of the piece.

Hephaestion cites this fragment, without a break, alongside another piece also traditionally attributed to Sappho; this accompanying quotation expresses the pains of the god Eros (*fr.* 130):

> Eros the loosener-of-limbs once again shakes me,
> that sweet-bitter, utterly irresistible little beast.

This particular representation of anguish was discussed in Chapter 2, but without reference to the fragment that follows (*fr.* 131). Hephaestion quotes both passages, without naming a poet, as an example of the same metre. Most editors now separate the pieces, although Eva-Maria Voigt printed them as one poem in her 1971 edition.[30] Voigt's Greek edition would therefore translate as follows:

> Eros the loosener-of-limbs once again shakes me,
> that sweet-bitter, utterly irresistible little beast.
> ... Atthis, the thought of me has become hateful to you,
> and you flee to Andromeda.

In the *Orations* of Maximus of Tyre (see Chapter 1), Andromeda is mentioned as a rival. Such biographical details offer tantalising options for a reconstruction of part of Sappho's life. It could be argued that Atthis was one of Sappho's favourite pupils, the relationship assumed a homo-erotic element, then Atthis broke Sappho's heart by absconding with a rival choral teacher, Andromeda. But such fictions, as inviting and as potentially helpful in the story of Sappho the 'lesbian' as they may appear to be, must be approached with caution.

There is simply no need to speculate about the possibilities of Sappho's lived experiences in preference to her poetic output. That she sang of a woman by the name of Atthis and that she loved her is surely enough. That this love may have entailed an erotic side is suggested, not only in *fragment* 96, but also in the following observation (*fr.* 49):

> I loved you a long time ago, Atthis, once ...
> a little child, without elegance, you seemed to me.

The textual history of this fragment, quoted in the above version by the Roman poet and grammarian, Terentianus Maurus (*c.* second century AD), is intriguing in that each line was also recorded separately, the first by Hephaestion in his *Handbook of Metres* and the second by Plutarch in his *Dialogue on Love*.[31] It could be posited that Plutarch interpreted the line as belonging to an *epithalamium* as he comments that Sappho was 'addressing a girl who was still too young for marriage'. Admittedly, the amount of Sappho's poetry available to Plutarch was surely more extensive than what remains today; nevertheless, once again, we simply do not know whether or not his observation is based on access to a greater volume of her work or whether it is speculation.

What is enlightening in this fragment – and more pertinent to an analysis of Sappho's erotics than fanciful biographical reconstructions – is her use of the verb *eraman* (here translated as 'I loved'). The verb has strong erotic connotations: expressly, it suggests 'being in love' or 'having a desire for'. Similarly, the intensity of the sexual feelings of the speaker in *fragment* 96 is shown by the inclusion of the noun *himeros* (*l.* 16), which also appears in *fragment* 31.5; this is a powerful word denoting sexual desire. These two words are the closest indicators, in the Sapphic corpus as we have it, of the transformation of romantic love into intense erotic yearning and realisation. In *eraman*, the speaker is clearly revealing that there was once a sexual aspect to the relationship with Atthis; by using the word *himeros*, the poet once again explicitly refers to the feelings of passionate or physical desire experienced by the absent woman towards Atthis.

In previous chapters other lyrics were examined in predominantly non-sexual contexts, yet pieces such as *poem* 1 (Chapter 2) and *fragment* 16 (Chapter 3) also lend themselves to the topic of Sapphic love. In the earlier discussion of *poem* 1, it was suggested that Sappho – in contradiction to some scholarly readings of the work – presents a decidedly 'male' approach to the female object of desire; namely, she pursues the woman in a discernibly aggressive way that suggests an adherence to the power dynamics entailed in ancient (male) relationships. The poem provides salient and additional insights into Sappho's attitude to erotic pursuit, here in the form of the hymnal or cletic style that defines her as a suppliant, praying to Aphrodite for release of frustrated desire. The cletic nature of *poem* 1 has been discussed in Chapter 2, and to this categorisation we may add the relatively new interpretation that posits the presence of an additional generic aspect, namely that of magical incantation. This is the suggestion of J.C.B. Petropoulos, who argues that the poem 'may well be a literary version – or even a "transcript" – of a type of love spell that was based on the cletic, or supplicatory, hymn'.[32] Petropoulos pays particular attention to lines 21-4 as indicators of 'a magical utterance'.[33] These contain part of Aphrodite's words to the desperate Sappho:

'And if she flees now, she will soon be chasing [you].
If she does not accept presents, she will give them.
If she does not love [you] now, soon she will,
even if she is not willing.'

The practice of magic was widespread in the ancient world and the preserved spells, primarily collected under the title of the *Greek Magical Papyri*, include written charms that are remarkably similar to *poem* 1 in both structure and vocabulary. In erotic spells, the divine addressee is often Aphrodite, who is invoked in a hymnal style but – in a manner more characteristic of spells – also commanded to assist the petitioner. Such a petitioner's imperative voice is evident in Sappho's poem, particularly in line 5 with the use of the verb *elthe* (literally, 'you come here!'), which encapsulates what may be defined as the 'entreaty-command'[34] evident in ancient spell formulae, although the use of the tone of command is indeed not as forceful here as it is in actual magical texts. Thus, Sappho may well have been inspired by the tradition of love spells, utilising them as a blueprint for poetic innovation.

In the sixth strophe (quoted above), identified by Petropoulos[35] and others as a particularly powerful use of magical discourse, Sappho incorporates the concept of 'binding', which is dominant in spell-casting, particularly in erotic contexts. The *Greek Magical Papyri* provide a multitude of such spells, in which the object of the petitioner's attraction is represented as being 'bound' to the will of the love-struck individual whose desperation incites them to magic, usually as a last recourse. Interpreted along such lines, Aphrodite's words at lines 21-4 point to the future success in binding the unnamed woman – the woman who will, as the goddess predicts, inevitably 'love' Sappho 'even if she is not willing' (*l.* 24).

Poem 1, read in part as an example of lyric spell-casting, reinforces the power dynamics that appear to be at play in some of Sappho's erotic verse. It is not wholly convincing to treat Sappho or the Sapphic voice as a precursor to the modern egalitarian lesbian. Sappho's world is not ours: it is an Archaic environment, patriarchal, one in which relationships, be they between women and men, or between members of the same sex, are governed by a gendered and social hierarchy that – although not as extremely differentiated as in the Classical era – nevertheless involved an approach to romantic unions or otherwise that assumed active and passive participants. It was also a world in which magic, a practice that was not regarded as necessarily oppositional to religion, operated to redress perceived power imbalance.

In contrast to the tone of determined pursuit in *poem* 1, *fragment* 16 is neither as erotically charged nor imbued with religious motif, but rather a romantic reverie about an absent loved one. Nor does *fragment* 16 have the desperation of *fragment* 31; indeed it is closer in tenor or poetic attitude to the nominated Sapphic voice of *fragment* 94, which calmly reminisces, and also recalls *fragment* 96 in its gentle eroticism. In this sense, *fragment* 16, when situated alongside *fragments* 94 and 96, and contrasted with *poem* 1 and *fragment* 31, reveals a dual theme in the works dealing with female-female love; namely, those about separation from loved ones and those that express the intensity of love at first sight or new love.

Fragment 16 does, however, share a literary technique with *fragment* 31, namely the emphasis on the evocation of the erotic gaze. In both pieces, Sappho conveys the image of someone (the raconteur) watching someone else (the object of desire and/or the beloved). For example, in *fragment* 16 (*ll.* 17-20) the singer recalls an image of the body of Anactoria:

> I would prefer to gaze upon her
> lovely walk and the glowing sparkle of her
> face than all the chariots of the Lydians and their
> armies.

Similarly, in *fragment* 31 (*ll.* 7-8), the theme of the narratorial gaze is evoked, albeit in a more general way:

> For just gazing at you for a second, it is impossible
> for me even to talk

Sappho prefers or desires to see Anactoria's walk and face rather than – as implied – virtually anything else. The verb *bolloiman* (*l.* 17) is in the optative mood, the particular inflected form of the verb indicating a wish or alternative conditional form that approximates in English as 'I would prefer'. Snyder comments that 'the mood of the verb here … renders the singer's statement a timeless one'.[36] While not overtly erotic, *bolloiman* does assume such a meaning because of its apposition to the adjective *eraton*, meaning 'lovely', 'charming' or 'beloved'. The latter word recalls the erotically-charged verb that ends the first stanza, *eratai* (translated here as 'loves'), and is indeed etymologically connected to it. *Eratai* usually means 'to be in love with' (as discussed above, in relation to *eraman*, an imperfect or past tense form of the same verb), and Sappho's use of the verb represents a passion for Anactoria in general – although the adjective applies only to her 'lovely walk' (*l.* 18).

Sappho would also prefer to see the 'glowing sparkle' of Anactoria's face than anything else. This image combined with that of Anactoria's gait renders Sappho's gaze as intense, observant, specifically directed to create the impression of her as an intimate observer and an observer of intimate features. Such particulars indicate, as does the presence of reverie, that the singer and the woman being 'sung' have shared an intense love; this contrasts to *fragment* 31's evocation of love at first sight and the complementary (and complimentary) gaze at the woman's overall beauty. In addition to the response to the sound of the object of desire (*l.* 5), the singer simply does not know where to look except everywhere (*ll.* 7-8).

The erotic power and effect of the gaze – both in reality and in the world of the poet – is recorded in *fragment* 23 (see Chapter 3) where the poet sings once more of looking at a woman (*fr.* 23.3-6):

(for when) I look at you face-to-face,
(not even) Hermione (seems) like you,
and to compare you to golden-haired Helen
(is not unwise).

Sappho's Helen may be the ultimate erotic icon for the woman who sings of other women.

The inducement of desire through the process of gazing at or observing another woman is relevant not only to the Sapphic 'I' but to other personae as well. In *fragment* 22, Sappho sings of Abanthis, whose desire for Gongyla is evoked through the image of the gaze (*fr.* 22.9-18):

... I bid you
sing of Gongyla, Abanthis,
taking the harp, while desire again
flies around and around you,   12

... the lovely woman. For the fold
of her garment, when you saw (it),
aroused you.
And I delight. For the blessed Cyprian   16

herself once blamed me ...
for praying ...

Sappho's advice to Abanthis, namely that desire (*pothos*) for
another woman should serve as the inspiration for lyric
composition, provides an insight into the poet's own artistic
motivation. Additionally, the fragment is erotic by implication; it is not Gongyla's clothing per se that is the source of
Abanthis' attraction but more likely the way the folds of the
clothing accentuate her body. The use of the noun *pothos*
augments the erotic mood of the fragment, suggesting as it
does desire, longing and yearning. We may also suggest that
the reference to Aphrodite, the 'Cyprian' (*l.* 16), adds to the
eroticism, but the piece is too damaged to allow us to take
this reading further.

Sappho also links the predicament of Abanthis with herself
through the use of the adverb *deute* (again) at line 11, a move
which is not unique to the poet, being part of 'one of the
commonest formulas in the surviving corpus of Archaic
Greek verse'.[37] *Deute* recurs several times in the Sapphic
corpus, especially in her hymn to Aphrodite, *poem* 1, in
which the adverb appears three times (and is perhaps alluded
to at *fr.* 22.16-18). Skinner describes Sappho's self-represen-
tation – or the representation of the Sapphic voice – as that
of the 'onlooker', the one who enjoys sharing the experience
of Abanthis. In this sense, the theme of the poet as observer,
as the gazer, is again present as 'the speaker at this present

moment apparently invokes the goddess while identifying vicariously with the love-sick Abanthis'.[38]

The Sapphic singer not only observes others but also observes herself, a poetic motif illustrated in *fragment* 58. This phenomenon too is situated in erotic contexts involving other women. We witness this theme most powerfully in *fragment* 31, in which the singer describes herself as gazing at the woman in question (*ll.* 7-8), being cognisant of the male who observes the same woman (*ll.* 1-5), and also hyper-aware of herself (*ll.* 7ff.). This intense self-awareness is evoked as if the singer is in fact observing or gazing at herself. It is as if she is watching from above or seeing a mirror image. Yet, ironically, she tells us that her 'eyes see nothing at all' (*l.* 11) and the reactions she experiences are almost all bodily sensations not requiring sight to acknowledge, with the possible exception being the reference to herself as 'more greenish than grass' (*ll.* 14-15). Nevertheless, the overall fragment conveys the scene as a visual experience (admittedly combined with physical responses), and Eva Stehle, in her study of the Sapphic gaze, comments on the singer's self-observation, beginning at lines 14-16:

> The narrator's gaze has shifted from the other woman to herself. With her new focus she observes herself both from within and from without. The audience too must shift from the simple position of 'looking' at another to the ambiguous position of both sharing the narrator's experience and watching her.[39]

The ancient Greeks believed that erotic passion, desire and love entered a person literally through the eyes. While there is doubt as to when this tenet began – and its most powerful expression does not find a voice until Plato's *Phaedrus* (255a-

257a)[40] – Sappho's contemporary, Ibycus of Rhegium, writing in the first half of the sixth century BC, clearly acknowledges the idea (*fr.* 287C.1-4):

> Eros again from beneath dark
>> eyelids darting me a melting look
> with spells of all kinds cast me
>> into the inextricable snares of the Cyprian.

Here, Ibycus is writing of Eros' infection: the god sends the poet a powerful glance that functions as a spell – similar, we may conjecture, to the evil eye of ancient folk tradition. This glance induces erotic desire that is conveyed metaphorically through the image of the poet being cast into the nets of Aphrodite or, more literally, into a passionate emotional state.

Sappho's emphasis on the gaze may therefore point towards an acknowledgement of this cultural tradition. Indeed, the image of *eros* entering an individual through the eyes functions as a powerful expression of the immediacy and shock of passion, while also emphasising the impact of the sight of the object of desire or, as Sappho sings, the sight of 'the most beautiful / thing on the dark earth' (*fr.* 16.2-3). On a related theme, she sings of grace (*charis*) pouring forth from the eyes, in a small fragment preserved by Athenaeus[41] (*fr.* 138, *c.* 200 AD):

> Stand ... if you are a beloved,
> and spread about that grace in [your] two eyes.

The Sapphic gaze, so gracefully and also, at times, so unsettlingly, described within the lyrics of love, desire, eroticism and friendship, is a significant component of her response to women. This, combined with the evocation of sensual responses, those of aroma and touch, is the means through which the poet expresses her love of women in all its intricacies and multiplicities.

5

Marriage Hymns

The discussion of the love of women in Chapter 4 raises the issues of the Sapphic 'voice' and the identity or identities of the singer(s) of the songs. Of significance to this topic is the use of the personal pronoun *egô* ('I'). In addition, we should be reminded that the inflected Greek language indicates the 'person' of the verbal subject ('I', 'he', 'she', 'it', etc.). Therefore we know that Sappho constructs songs from the perspective of the subjective 'I', although how subjective or personal her songs were intended to be remains a source of contention. Charles Segal perhaps best encapsulates the dilemma and offers a solution:

> In the case of Sappho … we cannot be sure where to draw the line between the personal and the conventional. It is not necessarily the unique but the recurrent and universal features of her experience of love that Sappho seeks to present. The formalised patterns of her language may, in fact, have served to link her own emotional life to situations of frequent and repeated occurrence in the culture or subculture to which she belonged.[1]

The marriage hymns or *epithalamia*, however, do not pose such problems in regard to the identity of the poetic voice. These songs, composed and performed for nuptial occasions, represent a public or traditional approach to the subject matter and we may assume that the personal voice of the poet is consequently subsumed. Nevertheless, Sappho produced some individualistic work which, once again, reveals her interest in the status of women; here specifically, the bride. Furthermore, as ancient choirs included performances by soloists, Sappho may have sung some of the lyrics herself.

Information on Archaic marriage traditions is essentially gleaned from the literature of the time. In Chapter 3, the poem on the marriage of Andromache and Hector was discussed, predominantly in terms of Sappho's utilisation of the Homeric epics, yet *fragment* 44 also provides details on wedding ceremonies. The 'opening' line of the fragment, for example, mentions Cyprus and we may infer from this reference to the birthplace of Aphrodite that the presence of the goddess of desire, passion and fertility was invoked during the celebration. The scene then shifts to refer to the process by which the bride-to-be, Andromache, is escorted to her new community (*ll.* 6-9), indicating that the bride would reside in her husband's precinct and, by implication, become part of his family. Additionally, the 'many golden bracelets and purple robes, / ornate delights, innumerable silver cups and ivory' (*ll.* 9-11) suggest the custom of bride price or dowry. But the principal theme of the fragment is the wedding celebration per se, as Sappho conveys the lively atmosphere of what we may assume to be a wedding in Archaic Mytilene: the community is involved, including women and virgins; the people are transported to the township via carts (the vehicles that transport the bride and key female members of the bridal party to the customary banquet); and wine, 'myrrh and cassia and frankincense' are mentioned (*l.* 30) – presumably for sacrifices to the gods to ensure their blessing. Music and song comprised a major element in the festivities (*ll.* 24-7) and involved various members of the community, apparently grouped in choirs based on age and gender. Some of the lyrics were in honour of the gods – in this instance, Apollo (*l.* 33) – as well as in praise of the bride and groom (*l.* 34).

Similarly, Alcaeus' *fragment* 42, also discussed in Chapter 3, provides several pieces of information on Archaic weddings, although, like Sappho's *fragment* 44, it is set in mythical times. Of importance to the topic at hand is Alcaeus' reference at lines 7-8 to the bride's departure from her homeland and her subsequent life in the territory of her husband.[2] As Andromache leaves her parental land at Thebe, so Thetis is taken from the halls of her father, Nereus. The communal atmosphere attested by Sappho is also conveyed by Alcaeus in his mythical wedding scene with the reference to 'all the holy gods' (*l.* 9) being invited to the celebration. The importance of the bride's purity is also signified by Alcaeus who describes Peleus untying 'the pure virgin's girdle' (*l.* 10). The latter phrase is redolent with significant bridal language: the noun *zoma* (usually in the form *zônê* in Classical Greek) is the standard word for the bridal belt (here translated as 'girdle'), the removal of which was a tradition on the night of the actual consummation. The virgin is the *parthenos*, also a traditional and specific term,[3] and her purity is reinforced by the adjective *hagna*, describing something that is pure, chaste and even holy. As the primary aim of marriage was to join families for various political, social and financial reasons and to ensure the birth of an heir, Alcaeus emphasises the legitimacy of the union between Peleus and Thetis by reference to the birth of a son (*l.* 13).

5. Marriage Hymns

In combination, these two fragments reveal a basic outline of some of the procedures and components of an Archaic wedding:

(a) there was a ceremonial journey to the site of the celebration (traditionally held at the house of the bride's father);
(b) festivities followed and involved both male and female kin and members of the community;
(c) at the gathering there were offerings to the gods and marriage hymns performed by both male and female choirs;
(d) at the conclusion of the banqueting and celebration the bride was escorted to the home of her spouse (here the more risqué *epithalamia* may have been recited; see below);
(e) there, with the bridal chamber prepared, the couple retired and, behind closed doors, the *zônê* would have been untied.

Epithalamia were clearly an important part of these proceedings and involved praise of the newly-weds. Not surprisingly, Sappho's eye for female beauty lends itself to some charming, if possibly conventional, compliments to the bride:

... chamber ...
... a bride with beautiful feet ... (*fr.* 103B)

(Sing of) the bride with the beautiful feet (*fr.* 103.4-5)

Bridegroom, there has never been a girl like this one (*fr.* 113)

The focus on the bride's feet is a conventional one. In the *Iliad*, for example, Hera is described as placing 'beautiful sandals' on her 'shiny feet' (14.186). Hesiod also describes females as 'beautiful-ankled' (*Theogony ll.* 507, 950), which indicates the continuation of this descriptive tradition. While we may not generally think to praise a woman's feet today, particularly those of a bride, in antiquity such praise was not uncommon and indeed, in a social context, flattering. The delicacy of a woman's feet suggests a life of ease and leisure, an indoor lifestyle indicating aristocratic heritage (or divinity) in the ages of Homer, Hesiod and Sappho. During the late Republic, Catullus continued the tradition, equating his beloved Lesbia with a goddess who walked upon a threshold with the 'delicate tread' (*poem* 68.70) of her 'resplendent sole' (*l.* 71). In contrast, *fragment* 113 gives an overall impression of female beauty by, ironically, specifying the uniqueness of the bride. Perhaps the fragment continued and described the woman in question, or perhaps, still maintaining her Homeric heritage, Sappho kept to the convention whereby physical details were kept to a minimum in order to convey the concept of universal beauty.

The most detailed portrait of a bride from the Sapphic *epithalamia* is as follows (*fr.* 112):

Joyful bridegroom, your marriage has reached the fruition
for which you prayed; you have the virgin for whom you
    prayed …
your body is graceful, your eyes …
are soft, and *eros* flows over your beautiful face
… Aphrodite gave much honour to you.

5. Marriage Hymns

Here Sappho encapsulates the overall joy and beauty presumably required in *epithalamia*. Although marriages were arranged in antiquity, Sappho romanticises the union by stating that the groom prayed for his bride, which by implication suggests that he fell in love with her. Likewise, the bride is shown as equally smitten as '*eros* flows over' her 'beautiful face' (*l.* 4). In terms of the aristocratic societies of Archaic and Classical Greece, such a suggestion may seem out-of-kilter as segregation of the sexes was the rule; but Sappho's Mytilene may well have differed from other social structures in this respect. If we recall *fragment* 31 and reject the interpretation that the scene must have been based on a marriage ceremony (because that would have been the only environment in which men and women could associate) there is the possibility – based on shaky evidence to be sure – that during the Archaic era the sexes did mix more on this island than they did elsewhere. Perhaps then, Sappho's couple really were in love, despite the marriage having been arranged. Perhaps they met at an unspecified event such as the one the poet herself depicts in *fragment* 31.

This is a fanciful reading of *fragment* 112, for in all likelihood Sappho is, as mentioned previously, simply romanticising the occasion as required. The whimsical interpretation is, however, an effective exercise in assessing the poet's ability to create an idealistic image of the bridal pair. In addition to alluding to the couple's mutual love, Sappho continues the romanticism through reference to the bride's beautiful body, soft eyes, and the presence of *eros* – here perhaps the physical incarnation of passion – literally drenching her face. She concludes the hyperbole with the ultimate compliment: Aphrodite herself honours her. What is interesting about the representation of the bride in this piece is the emphasis placed on her passion – her connection with *eros* – as opposed to that of the groom. While the latter is depicted as somewhat more restrained, having prayed for this particular *parthenos*, she is clearly the more sexualised and sexual persona, a reading furthered by the intimate association between her and Aphrodite. While Sappho's male contemporaries tended also to sexualise women, contending that they were more insatiable than men in order to condemn rather than flatter them,[4] she presents her bride as radiant in her sensuality and passion.

This representation of a young woman's sexuality is also conveyed in the following fragment, often defined as part of a wedding song, in which female desire is dramatised (*fr.* 102):

> Oh sweet mother, I am not able to weave at the loom,
> by desire I am overwhelmed for a boy because of slender
>   Aphrodite.[5]

The use of the powerful noun *pothos* (desire)[6] stresses the intensity of the sexual feelings. This overt expression of womanly eroticism, albeit gentle in its evocation of a burgeoning awareness, is the distinguishing factor of what may be described as a uniquely female voice in the poetry of Sappho. This is not to argue that as a woman Sappho exhibits an exclusive feminine essence that manifests itself in a language that is demonstrably and discernibly feminine, rather that her words represent a disruption of the established male discourse whereby women are defined according to social norms, namely as passive and, if sexually aware, possessed of a hyper-sexuality, destructive in nature. In a paper that examines the female 'voice' of

Sappho, Skinner encapsulates this decidedly *female* quality of the poet:

> While Sappho's manipulation of verbal devices like diction, figures of speech, and imagery is clearly indebted to the mainstream tradition ... her modes of subjectivity differentiate her to an extraordinary degree from her male counterparts – particularly those working within the same genre, whether *partheneion* [maiden song] or erotic monody.[7]

Such a concise analysis of the Sapphic 'voice' elucidates the poet's approach to the Homeric genre, for example, whereby she reveals the literary debt but in a way that also signals her individualistic departure from the tradition. In terms of her marriage hymns or, for that matter, her erotic monodies, Sappho's specifically 'womanly' perspective, which chronicles and thereby unconsciously – or, perhaps, consciously – celebrates the female condition, marks her work as distinctive, different, from her male contemporaries and predecessors.

As well as such gentle eroticism, ribaldry – sometimes present in contemporary wedding celebrations – was a feature of both Greek and Roman *epithalamia*. The rhetorical theorist Demetrius, on one of these bawdy songs, refers to Sappho making 'cheap fun' of the groom and the doorkeeper, regarding such lyrics as using 'commonplace rather than poetic language'.[8] Yet Demetrius does not consider the cultural background to this component of the *epithalamia*, in which the making of fun was possibly an invocation of fertility – hence the focus on lewd references – and/or a form of apotropaic ritual, namely the means by which an act is performed or words are vocalised or recorded in order to avert divine or supernatural vengeance or spite. The ancient Greeks were aware of the prospect of the jealousy of the gods, and a marriage ceremony where the couple were joyous could provide an environment for divine spite; thus, by embarrassing the pair with rude jokes, the gods may be placated.

Indeed, Sappho is skilled at this type of humour, which as the surviving fragments reveal, was directed at the groom and also the doorkeeper. First the groom (*fr.* 111):

> Up with the roof,
> Hymenaeus!
> Get it up, workmen,
> Hymenaeus!
> The bridegroom
> approaches, on a par with Ares –
> bigger than a big man!

Sappho refers to Hymenaeus whose presence at the ceremony was customarily invoked to ensure a good omen for the couple. Hymenaeus was the god of both the wedding and the wedding song per se; here he is summoned to assist in the raising of a canopy over the marital proceedings. The fertility that is symbolically associated with Hymenaeus is accentuated by two phallic images: the physical raising of the canopy or roof (*l.* 1) and the comparison of the groom with Ares (*l.* 6) with the associated statement 'bigger than a big man' (*l.* 7). Ares is an appropriate reference in terms of phallic/fertility imagery; as the lover of Aphrodite and the god of war, Ares is a symbol of hyper-masculinity.

In marriages of the Greek upper-classes, the couple, on the

wedding night, would have been escorted to the bridal chamber and the entrance subsequently closed and guarded – hence the role of the doorkeeper. Presumably, the latter played a role in the ceremony prior to his role as security guard, possibly serving a comic and festive role, including being the focus of jibes. Here Sappho possibly refers to his alleged sexual capacity (*fr.* 110[a]):

> The feet of the doorkeeper are enormous,
> five oxen provided the leather for his sandals,
> and ten cobblers toiled in their making.

The euphemistic equation of the size of the doorkeeper's feet to the size of his penis appears to capture the style of the ribaldry of the *epithalamia*; sources such as Sappho and Catullus (also Theocritus writing in the third century BC) reveal that the humour is usually non-confrontational or non-explicit. Page suggests that these risqué verses were 'presumably recited by the assembly which went in procession from the bride's house to the bridegroom's after the ceremonial banquet'.[9] This statement, which offers a suggestive contextual placement for the fragment, reminds us of the various stages of the Greek marriage ceremony, and the prominence of processions to various locales. Alternatively, such songs may have been sung at the conclusion of the festivities when the couple reached the bridal chamber. At this point also, as Margaret Williamson[10] reminds us, the bride's friends feign an attempt at rescuing her (thus explaining the presence of the doorkeeper); a significant part of the overall wedding ritual is a continuation of the emphasis on the bride's innocence and, accordingly, her fear of what lies ahead. It may well be, then, that these young women were the actual performers of such naughty verse, as they are in Theocritus' 'Epithalamium to Helen' (*Idyll* 18).[11]

Sappho's interest in the world of the female is strongly evident in the *epithalamia*. Since a young woman was expected to remain a virgin until marriage, female purity was highly protected and much prized, as is evident in some of the imagery from Sappho's marriage songs. Indeed, a woman who lost her virginity prior to marriage was socially scorned and unlikely to find a husband.

Prior to Sappho, Hesiod,[12] for example, strongly suggests marriage to a virgin as opposed to a widow (*Works and Days* 695ff.):

> Bring a wife to your house when you are of the right age, 695
> not too short of thirty nor much older.
> This is the correct age for marriage.
> Your wife should have been an adolescent for four years,
>   and married to you in the fifth.
> Marry a virgin so you can train her in good ways.
> Be careful to marry one living near you,
>   and be aware of all around you.   700
> Ensure the marriage is not a joke to your neighbours:
> a man wins nothing better than a good wife,
> and again, he wins nothing worse than a bad wife –
> [the one] greedy for food, who roasts her man without fire,
> strong though he is, and brings to him permanent
>   old age.   705

This passage provides an unambiguous attitude to the process of choosing a wife, and although Hesiod lived approximately a generation at least before Sappho, his attitude towards women and marriage is indicative – generally speaking – of the Archaic mindset, particularly among the growing bourgeois class. Besides the stress on the right type of bride, the passage emphasises the preferred age gap between husband and wife. In marriages of the Archaic and Classical ages, this differentiation is more or less standard, although little evidence is available for the practice on Lesbos. Interestingly, however, one of Sappho's fragments reveals that the poem's female speaker, at least, did not regard marriage to a younger man as appropriate (*fr.* 121):

> But if you are my loved one,
> take the bed of a younger woman,
> for in a partnership I will not
> endure being the elder.

Stobaeus (fifth century AD), who records the piece in his *Anthology*, prefaces it with the following: '… in marriage the age of the partners should be considered'.[13] Perhaps the singer is here voicing an individualistic perspective or perhaps she is reflecting an opinion that was socially constructed.

Perhaps the best known fragments of Sapphic *epithalamia* are two separate pieces that appear to place emphasis on the chastity of the bride-to-be; possibly from the one song, they may be interpreted as illustrative of counsel to young women:

> As the honey-apple reddens at the furthest point of the
>   bough,
> at the furthest point of the highest bough, the apple-pickers
>   have forgotten it;
> no, not really forgotten it, but could not reach it. (*fr.* 105[a])

Like the hyacinth that shepherds in the mountains
tread upon, and on the ground the purple blossom ...
  (*fr.* 105[c])

The first piece was preserved in Syrianus' commentary on Hermogenes' *On Forms*;[14] the second, quoted by Demetrius[15] without an author or context, has been assigned to Sappho because of its resemblance to the fragment from Syrianus in both metre (the Homeric dactylic hexameter) and structure (primarily the use of simile). In Syrianus' commentary, the implicit bridal imagery of *fragment* 105(a) is noted:

> It was the habit of Sappho to compare the bride to an apple: so inviting to those eager to pluck her before the correct season that they all but taste her with the tip of their fingers, and also to him who wants to pluck the apple in due season that he watches for the peak of loveliness ...[16]

In both fragments, Sappho – in a far more subtle way – is essentially repeating Hesiod's heavy-handed outcry: 'Marry a virgin so you can train her in good ways' (*Works and Days, l.* 698). If we assume the fragments come from *epithalamia*, Sappho assumes the didactic role – perhaps as actual choral leader or monodist – and advises the young women present to protect their virginity. She utilises the image of the apple (*fr.* 105[a]) and the hyacinth (*fr.* 105[c]) as the poetic tools of this instruction: the woman who keeps her virginity until marriage is likened to the apple at the 'furthest point of the bough', while the one who forfeits it is compared to the despoiled flower.[17]

Here Sappho marks a departure from Hesiod on the

subject of female virginity: whereas he stresses the public necessity for a male to make the correct *choice* of wife ('Ensure the marriage is not a joke to your neighbours', *l.* 701), she relates the topic to the female per se, speaking to the female audience in terms of caring for – essentially respecting – their own bodies.

While Syrianus' commentary specifies that *fragment* 105(a) comes from a marriage hymn and equates the bride, and thereby virginity, with the apple, *fragment* 105(c) has also been interpreted and categorised similarly through comparison with Catullus' *epithalamium, poem* 62. In the latter, Catullus, most likely following once again in the poetic footsteps of Sappho (yet with significant reinterpretations), has his chorus of young women sing of the state of feminine virginity through reference to a flower (*poem* 62.39-48):

As a flower blossoms, concealed in a sheltered garden,
unknown to the herd, torn up by no plough,   40
which the winds caress, the sun strengthens, the rain
    nourishes;
many boys have desired it, many girls:
when that very flower has faded, plucked by an elegant nail,
no boys long for it, no girls:
thus a virgin, as long as she remains intact, so long is she
    dear to her kindred;   45
when, with body defiled, she has lost her chaste flower,
she remains neither delightful to boys, nor dear to girls.
Hymen, Hymenaeus, Hymen let you come, Hymenaeus![18]

While Catullus' version makes evident his debt to Sappho, his alteration – combining both of her fragments in the one refrain – anticipates a response in the form of counter-argument by the chorus of young men (*poem* 62.49-58b):

> As the unwed vine that grows in a treeless field,
> never lifts itself up, never nourishes the ripe grape,   50
> but bending down its slender body with descending weight
> now, now just about touches the furthest point with its
>   root;
> this one no farmers, no oxen have tilled:
> but, if by chance that same vine is married to a husband
>   elm,
> that one many farmers, many oxen have tilled: 55
> thus, as long as a virgin remains intact, so long will she
>   age uncultivated;
> when, at the right time, she has acquired an appropriate
>   marriage,
> she is more dear to the man and less a nuisance to the
>   parent.
> Hymen, Hymenaeus, Hymen let you come, Hymenaeus!

Catullus' male chorus refutes the girls' argument – inspired by Sappho's idealisation of the precious apple and the sullied flower – by stressing that a seemingly unattainable bride-to-be runs the risk of remaining in a perpetual state of virginity, ageing without cultivation.

Eva Stehle Stigers comments on the Catullan re-visioning while simultaneously providing some insightful interpretations of the Sapphic original:

> The new image misrepresents the poignant and paradoxical reality to which Sappho was giving expression in both her images. In the first place, Sappho's flower image conveyed the

116

vulnerability of the girl who combined innocence with openness to sexual experience. But Catullus' girls feel none of the
tension centred in Sappho's flower image because they feel (or
admit) no openness to passion.[19]

Catullus' flower imagery may, as Stehle argues, misrepresent
the two pieces on which it is based, but deliberately so;
perhaps 'reinterpret' is a preferable definition of his process of
imitation. Stehle is correct, however, in her argument that
Catullus' maidens are opposed to marriage and, by implication, 'passion'; hence the reply of the young men at lines
49-58b. The precious flower in the cultivated garden in *poem*
62 is dramatically different to Sappho's hyacinth-maiden
growing wild on the mountainside and vulnerable to the
intrusion of men. Yet while *fragment* 105(c) may be suggestive of a female passion, or at least sexual curiosity, Sappho
sings of the loss of virginity in a way that stresses desecration.
To be sure, the social implications underlie the fragment, but,
as previously suggested, Sappho's interest in female sexuality
per se points to a reading of the fragment as a message to the
parthenoi present at the wedding banquet, to honour their
virginity as one would a precious flower or, more ideally, trea-
sure it as a shining, plump apple, ripe for plucking – but only
at the right time.

Sappho's intense awareness of the importance of a young
woman's self-image, status and even power as *parthenos* is
further suggested in the following piece (*fr.* 107):

Do I still yearn for virginity?

This small remnant perhaps best encapsulates the poet's
perspective on virginity as a sexual state that is of acute signif-

icance to young women. The straightforward question, which may well be rhetorical, stresses the hyper-awareness of a young woman in respect to her status as a virgin. On a similar theme is the voice of the maiden who addresses her virginity and receives a reply (*fr.* 114):

Nymphê:
'Virginity (*parthenia*), virginity, where have you gone,
    leaving me?'
Parthenia:
'No more will I come to you, no more will I come.'

This fragment, with its dialogue structure (designed for a double chorus), may be as unfamiliar to us as the previous one in respect of the concepts it presents. It conveys once more the significance of female virginity in the ancient Greek world, which is revealed in two ways: the personification of virginity, and the awareness of the *nymphê* or bride that virginity, once lost, is irredeemable. The power of the words is inherent in the sexual constructs of the time, namely that the female was at her most desirable when she was a *parthenos* – most especially when she was literally at the point of marriage – a bride; hence the tone of trepidation in the young woman's question and the definitive answer she receives (an answer she already knows). This social and psychological reality thereby explains why the virgins of the *epithalamia* are sensual and sexual beings and are thereby depicted with the imagery of flowers and fruit, both of which emphasise beauty, freshness and ripeness. This state of existence, however, is as transitory as the blossoms and apples themselves, and once it ends so too does its essential desirability. Once deflowered, the bride – whose wedding marks a transitional or liminal state-of-being – enters a new way of life and a new status, that of wife and mother, and these roles do not allow her a sensual identity.

The last fragments for discussion in this chapter have been preserved in the *Oxyrhynchus Papyri*. First *fr.* 27:

... for once, were you also a child   4
...come now, sing of these things

...

you grant us grace;   7

for we are going to a wedding; and you
also (know) this indeed; but send away
the virgins as fast as you can, may the gods
have ...   11

... no road to great Olympus
... for mortals ...   13

This fragment is not definitively accepted by scholars as deriving from a marriage hymn although the fact that it seems composed for a chorus and refers to a wedding (*l.* 8) suggests the possibility.[20] The identity of the addressee is also in doubt as what remains does not indicate any gender; for example, the word for child, *pais* (*l.* 4), can be either masculine or feminine.[21] The reference to grace (*charis*) may have involved a passage on Aphrodite, a deity regularly connected with *epithalamia*, but as we know from Sappho's own poetry, not strictly so. Also uncertain are lines 9-10 that refer to the driving away of the *parthenoi*; one viable interpretation, assuming the marriage context, is the ritual attempts at disassociating the bride from her female companions as the ceremony progressed from the final stages of the pre-wedding ritual to the actual banquet room for the formal feast and prelude to consummation.

Fragment 30 is equally as problematic in terms of its subject matter, although the wedding context is slightly more evident:

Night ...

Virgins ...
all through the night ...
may we sing of the love between you
and the purple-girdled bride.

But come, awaken;
go (to) the unmarried youths of your own age,
that we may see (less) sleep than (the bird?)
of the clear song.

This seems to have been composed for a female chorus as the groom, or what appears now to be the husband, is bidden to wake from the bridal chamber and search out unmarried men his own age (namely those who were once his peers). The reason for this imperative is apparently so the chorus can continue singing – singing of the love between the married couple. Interestingly, the Greek noun *eros* has been replaced by the more formal and less passionate, *philotês*, which is more socially appropriate to a husband and wife.

Such a nuanced shift in vocabulary is highly sensitive on the part of the poet. While we acknowledge that Sappho is here fulfilling her role on a public level, her perceptions, finely honed from her other lyric life as a monodist, remind us that perhaps always in matters of *eros*, Sappho knows it does not last forever. Perchance, however, we could expect it to last more than one night; perhaps she believed it did ... between women.

Farewell, bride, farewell, honoured groom. (*fr.* 116)

6

Debts to Sappho

In Chapter 1, the negative or anxious responses to Sappho's sexuality were discussed alongside some of the more recent trends in her biographical tradition. While that chapter dealt primarily with various accounts of the poet's life, and focused on the ancient and early modern European periods, this chapter turns to the debts to Sappho – the reception of her life and words – by artists, poets, gender 'politicians', feminists and lesbians. This is a truly ambitious undertaking as her influence was evident in antiquity and continues to be a steadfast force in twenty-first-century arts and humanities circles. This selection is therefore based on personal preference and on some of the more widely acknowledged inheritors of the Sapphic tradition. Throughout the book, we have turned to Catullus and his imitations of the Sapphic voice. Catullus, then, seems to be a most appropriate starting point.

In the Roman educational tradition, boys and young men from financially secure families were schooled in the reading of the Greek canon, among which the works of Homer, Sappho and later authors of all genres were included. The pedagogical justification behind the rigorous training in rhetoric, moral and philosophical tenets, was to produce civilised future citizens. Catullus, a member of the local aristocracy of Verona, was well schooled in such a fashion as his poetry reflects an almost phenomenal grasp of

and familiarity with both the Greek and Latin literary
annals. In addition to the significant influence of the
Hellenistic or Alexandrian School (Greek writers from the
third to the first centuries BC), Catullus acknowledges the
influence of (especially) Homer and Sappho. In Chapter 4,
his most direct homage to Sappho, *poem* 51, was discussed
in relation to its source, *fragment* 31. In this Latin
reworking of the Greek original, Catullus changes the
gender of the speaker and casts himself as the tortured
singer who gazes at the object of desire. Furthermore, unlike
Sappho, Catullus names himself as the singer and casts his
'mistress', Lesbia, in the role of Sappho's unnamed woman,
alterations that enhance the personal tone of the work.
Moreover, Catullus signposts his debt by rendering his
poem in Sapphic metre, the lyric verse she supposedly
invented or at least perfected. This metre appears in only
one other poem by Catullus, *poem* 11, in which he has
echoed Sappho's *fragment* 105(c) in the closing stanza
(*ll.* 21-4):

> and let her not, as before, look for my love,
> which, due to her fault, has fallen like the flower of the
> furthest point of the field, after it has been touched
> by the plough passing by.[1]

As Sappho compares a despoiled young woman to a trampled
hyacinth, Catullus compares his *amor* to the flower damaged
by the plough (a symbol of Lesbia and her ruthless sexuality
and insensitivity). If we examine the lines more closely, there
is also the possibility that he has combined the complementary Sapphic lines, namely *fragment* 105(a), in which the
highly prized virgin is likened to an apple on the highest

bough. Catullus is the flower on 'the furthest point of the field' (*ll.* 22-3).

Sappho's influence on Catullus has been discussed by scholars for well over a hundred years, and it is regularly acknowledged that the (at times) distinctive feminine voice found in his poetry is partly an attempt to capture, to recreate the intensity, the emotion of the Sapphic originals. By 'feminine voice' I do not mean that Catullus attempts to feign femininity but rather to express emotional desolation and a sense of powerlessness through an equation with the delicacy and passivity of the woman and her symbolic world, that of the floral (*poem* 11), that of the visceral (*poem* 51). Thus, in the patriarchal environment of late Republican Rome, Catullus' understanding and experience of *amor*, the Latin equivalent of the Greek *eros*, whether real or poetically imagined, at times lead him to envision himself as the Sapphic persona – a voice that regularly sings of the passivity of one rendered helpless by love.

While Catullus was clearly unconcerned with Sappho's sexuality, preferring to acknowledge her poetic brilliance and her role as one of his Muses, so to speak, his fellow Latin poets were not quite as consistently reverential. Horace's ambiguous 'masculine Sappho', discussed in the Introduction, may imply a pejorative response to her sexuality, and Ovid's *Heroides* 15 was the major source for the rejection of Sappho as a lover of women from the early modern European age onwards. Yet both poets clearly admired her work.

Horace mentions Sappho in several odes, including *Ode* 2.13.24-5, a humorous piece in which the poet describes a near-death experience when a tree on his Sabine farm falls, barely missing him. The mishap inspires Horace's musings on death and the multiplicity of its possible manifestations. He also contemplates the land of the dead and presents a short but vivid image of Sappho, singing – or more accurately, bewailing – the girls from her homeland, the implication being that they have not returned her love. While we may argue that Horace has, indirectly, assimilated the already established image of Sappho as the archetypal jilted lover – an image quite possibly nuanced by her sexuality – he does at least acknowledge her alongside Alcaeus (*ll.* 26ff.) in the land of the blest. Yet Horace's respect for Sappho seems not exactly one of parity with Alcaeus, as D.A. Campbell acknowledges:

> What is most interesting and surprising is the treatment of Sappho and unfavourable comparison with Alcaeus: not only does Sappho get a brief two lines, factual and cold, whereas Alcaeus has three ... Horace goes out of his way to add that, although both arouse admiration down there, it is Alcaeus who draws the crowd with his poems of battle and the expulsion of tyrants.[2]

In *Ode* 4.9 Horace offers a defence of the lyric genre; admittedly the epics of Homer are truly great, but lyricists such as Stesichorus (640-555 BC), Alcaeus, Pindar (522-443 BC) and Simonides (556-469 BC) are, in the context of their own genre, equally inspirational. Sappho, again, joins her male peers (*Ode* 4.9.10-12):

> ... thus far the love
> of the Aeolian girl still breathes and with this key
>   her passions still live in faithfulness.

Thus Horace emphasises Sappho's eternal brilliance, a poetic honour he hoped one day would be applied to himself.[3]

Ovid is especially enamoured with the poetry of Sappho, as seen in the exhortation from *Ars Amatoria* (*The Art of Love*), Book 3, in which he urges women to read several Greek poets, including Sappho: 'and let Sappho be known [to you] (for what is more erotic than that?)' (*l.* 331). In the *Remedia Amoris* (*The Cures for Love*), Ovid admits: 'Me – certainly – did Sappho make better for [my] mistress' (*l.* 761), while in *Tristia* (*Sorrows*), he proclaims: 'What did Sappho teach the Lesbian girls, if not to love?' (2.365). In each of these three instances, Ovid refers to Sappho as a poet-educator, a woman whose work taught her 'pupils' – both in her lifetime and afterwards – the art of love. Ovid's respect for the genius of Sappho is also evident when we consider these quotations in context, for in each relevant section, he situates the Sappho reference alongside other great Greek poets, most commonly Callimachus (*c.* 280-245 BC), one of the most significant influences on the Latin poets of the late Republic and early Imperial ages. Finally, and perhaps the most poignant reference to Sappho, are the lines from *Tristia* Book 3, in which Ovid, desolate in his banishment from Rome, writes of (and to) his female protégé, Perilla (3.7.19-20):

> Thus, if the fires are still in your breast, as before,
> > only the female poet from Lesbos will surpass your work.

Reynolds, in her important compilation of Sapphic receptions, *The Sappho Companion*, states: 'For the Roman writers then Sappho was, at best, a poet of love; worse, a nymphomaniac; and, worst of all, a lover of women.'[4] This is somewhat of an exaggeration. While the works of Horace and Ovid may show traces of anxiety (particularly Ovid's *Heroides*

15, which sanitises Sappho's sexuality to the point of rendering her a neurotic), the pre-eminent image is one of poetic genius. In contrast, it would appear that the Greek response to her, beginning in approximately the fifth century BC, was more overtly hostile and ridiculing, but again this needs to be qualified in terms of genre: the images of her – particularly as a hyper-heterosexual, are from comedies.

In Chapter 1 the fragmentary state of the Sapphic corpus was discussed, with the conclusion that for now we simply cannot reach a definitive answer as to why her lyrics, along with countless other masterpieces from antiquity, effectively vanished. From what remains, we may cautiously posit that the era of her greatest appreciation in the ancient world was from the late Republic to early Imperial times. What happened between the laudations (and apprehension) of the Latin poets and the chroniclers of works such as the *Suda* remains as dim as the Dark Ages. What we do know, however, is that a resurgence of interest in the works of Sappho began in Europe in the sixteenth century. Thus, by the Renaissance, Sappho as a source of inspiration brought forth reworkings and reinterpretations of her poetry in a vein similar to the artistic tributes paid by Catullus, Horace and Ovid. So began the Sappho 'industry' once more, and it has not stopped since.

The critic or scholar is spoilt for choice when it comes to selecting material that illustrates the debt to Sappho. These range from poetic imitation and reformation to artistic interpretation to social, political and gender-based inspiration. One could begin with the earliest examples of Sapphic reference, which are not so much artistic or political revisionings as biographical re-assemblages freighted with cultural baggage that reveal more about the era in which they were produced, and quite possibly the individual authors, than about the poet herself. Boccaccio's *De Claris Mulieribus* and Pisan's *La Cité des Dames* recall in various ways the collected *Testimonia* of antiquity, respectively recasting Sappho as *the* notoriously clever woman and one of the female contradictions of the patriarchal law that women are intellectually inferior.

In addition to the reception of Sappho and her work by Lyly, Donne, Philips and Louÿs, Renaissance and post-Renaissance poets, artists and playwrights emulated her. Among the ardent followers of Sappho were the Victorians, and among these, one of the most passionate was Michael Field. In 'Atthis, My Darling', the last stanza reads:

> My darling! Nay, our very breath
> Not light nor darkness shall divide;
> Queen Dawn shall find us on one bed,
> Nor must thou flutter from my side
> An instant, lest I feel the dread,
> At this, the immanence of death.

The poet included this piece in the collection entitled *Long Ago* (1889), a series of Sappho-inspired poems also indebted to Henry Wharton's *Sappho: Memoir, Text, Selected Renderings, and a Literal Translation* (1885). 'An Invitation', from the collection *Underneath the Bough: A Book of Verse* (1893), further reveals Michael Field's empathetic response to the originals:

> Come and sing, my room is south;
> Come with thy sun-governed mouth,
>   Thou wilt never suffer drouth,
>   Long as dwelling
> In my chamber of the south ...

6. Debts to Sappho

There's a lavender settee,
Cushioned for my love and me;
    Ah, what secrets there will be
     For love-telling,
When her head leans on my knee!

Books I have of long ago
And today; I shall not know
Some, unless thou read them, so
    Their excelling
Music needs thy voice's flow ...

All the Latins *thou* dost prize!
Cynthia's lover by thee lies,
Note Catullus, type and size
    Least repelling
To thy weariable eyes.

And for Greek! Too sluggishly
Thou dost toil; but Sappho, see!
    And the dear Anthology
     For thy spelling.
Come, it shall be well with thee.

Michael Field was the combined *nom de plume* of aunt and niece, Katherine Bradley (1848-1914) and Edith Cooper (1862-1913) respectively, who lived as 'a closer married couple'[5] and, as evident from their creative output, literary celebrants of their chosen sexuality and lifestyle. Yopie Prins articulates the challenges inherent in an analysis of this exquisite, yet complex, poetic partnership: 'How shall we read these poems written by two women writing as a man writing as Sappho?'[6]

We can simply read these poems as erotic elegy, as poetry as effortless yet as psychologically intricate as the work of Sappho and as subversive female discourse. In the closing stanza of 'Atthis, My Darling' (see p. 128), the sheer ecstasy of love is evoked dramatically and in unadorned style with the use of the vocative: 'My darling!' The connection between love and death, characteristic of some of Sappho's most famous fragments, especially *fragments* 31 and 94 (on which it is loosely based), is here subtly explored. Neither light (life) nor death (darkness) shall separate the lovers' love (represented by the symbol of shared breath). Indeed, even the briefest separation is akin to death, reminding the lovers that they are indeed mortal and that the ultimate separation is inevitable.

In 'An Invitation', Sappho's ability to evoke details of feminine beauty – the sway of Anactoria's walk, or the indescribable beauty of Cleis' face (like flowers) – is recaptured in the image of the lover's 'sun-governed mouth' (*l.* 2), which suggests not only physical form but also sweetness of voice (and mouth). The evocation of a female and feminine environment, a 'chamber of the south' (*l.* 5), where there is 'a lavender settee' that is 'cushioned' (*l.* 7), recalls Sappho's depiction of Aphrodite's sensual grove (*fr.* 2) and the 'soft beds' of *fragment* 94. The shared eroticism and intellectualism of Sappho's poetry, namely the pieces that address females and/or express female environs, are also caught in the depiction of women reciting together in 'An Invitation'. Sappho's debt to Homer is matched by Michael Field's debt to other poets of antiquity; Propertius (*l.* 17), Catullus (*l.* 18) and, of course, the Tenth Muse herself (*l.* 22).

The ingenuity and beauty of Michael Field's poetry was

not, unfortunately, universal when it came to rewriting Sappho in the nineteenth century and beyond. There were more failures than successes when it came to artistic reception,[7] although the accomplished renditions are indeed memorable.

While poets, playwrights, novelists, painters and sculptors pondered Sappho, others chose to 'be' Sappho (or at least to model lives and communities on a personalised vision of her). The centre for Sapphism was Paris and later Mytilene. Among the most fascinating of the recreations of the Sapphic experience was the environment created by Renée Vivien (1877-1909), also known as the 'Muse of Violets' in honour of her love of flowers and her passion for her childhood friend, Violet Shilleto. A prolific novelist and poet, Vivien found an idealised expression of her sexuality in Sappho who, by the Victorian era, had become an icon and model for lesbians.

In addition to producing a wealth of literature inspired by Sappho (among others),[8] Vivien and her lover, Natalie Barney (1876-1972), travelled to Lesbos in an attempt to establish an artists' colony there in 1904, and although their goal was never achieved, Vivien continued to visit the island until her death. Barney also had previous desires – essentially realised – to emulate a Sapphic community in Paris. Her first Sapphic salon was in Neuilly and then in the Rue Jacob; at the latter, Barney created a Greek garden complete with temple, bust of Sappho and *chaise-longue*, and entertained various artists, novelists, intellectuals and lovers, including the French author, Colette. Reynolds enticingly describes the environment thus:

In her home she set about creating an island – *the* women's island – in the modern city. It was to be a nostalgic re-creation of Sappho's ancient home, and a celebration of the modern woman: free, independent, sensually loving, self-sufficient. Colette ... was seen sliding naked through the greenery. The Temple was lit up with candles and perfumed with incense. Poetry was read, music was played. Barney, Vivien and the rest dressed up as ladies and pages, as wood nymphs and shepherds, as the Loves and the Graces.[9]

Barney also wrote and produced, among other Sappho-inspired works, a play entitled *Équivoque* (which we could loosely translate as *Uncertainty*) about the life of Sappho, which she staged in her Greek garden in 1906.

The lives and literature of women such as Vivien and Barney are testimony to the significance of Sappho in the shaping of a lesbian identity during the Victorian era. To their generation, as well as to Michael Field, Sappho was a heroine of lesbian freedom and creative brilliance, of a female-centric lifestyle and a feminist prototype to emulate. And while their visions and re-visionings of Sappho are as clouded, distorted, personalised and politicised as those of their predecessors', their symbolic appropriation of the poet and her work attests to the female-female eroticism of her voice and, arguably, may well have contributed to the foundations of the gay liberation movement.

Yet lesbian advocates and early feminists were not the only devotees of Sappho, her sexuality and, most importantly, her poetry. Baudelaire was inspired by her art and her persona.[10] In 1857 he published *Les Fleurs du mal* (*Flowers of Evil*), a collection of a hundred poems, composed during the previous two decades. On various occasions, he proclaimed that the title would be *Les Lesbiennes*, and although this did not come to pass, three poems deal with this subject matter: 'Lesbos', 'Femmes damnées: Delphine et Hippolyte' ('Women Doomed: Delphine and Hippolyta') and 'Femmes damnées'. In 'Lesbos,' Baudelaire evokes Sappho through the island (stanza 5):

> Let old Plato look upon you with an austere eye;
> You earn pardon by the excesses of your kisses
> And the inexhaustible refinements of your love,
> Queen of the sweet empire, pleasant and noble land.
> Let old Plato look upon you with an austere eye.[11]

This objective, third-person narration is disrupted, however, when the poet himself enters the text and proclaims his inheritance of the Lesbian artistic tradition (stanzas 9-11):

> For Lesbos chose me among all other poets
> To sing the secret of her virgins in their bloom,
> And from childhood I witnessed the dark mystery
> Of unbridled laughter mingled with tears of gloom;
> For Lesbos chose me among her poets.
>
> And since then I watch from Leucadia's summit,
> Like a sentry with sure and piercing eyes
> Who looks night and day for tartane, brig or frigate,
> Whose forms in the distance flutter against the blue;
> And since then I watch from Leucadia's summit,
>
> To find out if the sea is indulgent and kind,
> If to the sobs with which the rocks resound
> It will bring back some night to Lesbos, who forgives,
> The worshipped body of Sappho, who departed
> To find out if the sea is indulgent and kind.

Baudelaire's identification with Lesbos – with Sappho – is open to debate: perhaps he is revealing an alignment with the condemned women, the lesbians, of which he writes; most certainly he is honouring Sappho as a source of artistic inspiration and, maybe, revealing a personal affinity with Sapphism per se, in keeping with the Decadent aesthetic.[12]

In 'Femmes damnées: Delphine et Hippolyte' we witness the erotically-charged dialogue between two female lovers, beginning with Delphine's words to Hippolyta (stanzas 7-10):

'Hippolyta, sweet, what do you think of our love?
Do you understand now that you need not offer
The sacred burnt-offering of your first roses
To a violent breath which could make them wither?

My kisses are as light as the touch of May flies
That caress in the evening the great limpid lakes,
But those of your lover will dig furrows
As a wagon does, or a tearing ploughshare;

They will pass over you like heavy teams
Of horses or oxen, with cruel iron-shod hooves …
Hippolyta, sister! please turn your face to me,
You, my heart and soul, my all, half of my own self,

Turn toward me your eyes brimming with azure and stars!
For one of those bewitching looks, O divine balm,
I will lift the veil of the more subtle pleasures
And lull you to sleep in an endless dream!'[13]

Baudelaire demonstrates his Classical learning by his choice of names: 'Hippolyta' is the name of the legendary Queen of the

Amazons, while 'Delphine' is an allusion to the Delphic Oracle, the great Sibyl of Apollo who resides at Delphi. Represented as a predatory, manipulative creature, Delphine exhibits a stereotypical feminine – or lesbian – form of sophistry in her attempts to convince Hippolyta that woman-woman love or, more precisely, her lesbian eroticism, is far superior to the rough encounters of the male. Hippolyta, more passive, more reticent in her fresh sexual awakening, is puzzled in a child-like way, asking Delphine: ' "Is there something strange in what we have done?" ' (stanza 13). The unfortunate Hippolyta, not exactly living up to her powerful name, thereby leaves herself open to Delphine's furious reply, which incorporates a defence of lesbianism.

Decadent that he is, Baudelaire's lesbians are grotesque caricatures envisioned through a shattering and voyeuristic male gaze. Even in his naïve or perhaps anxious defence of lesbian desire, the poet produces some ghastly and ethically impoverished platitudes that, although suitably Decadent, are also suitably Victorian. In the third poem on the subject, 'Femmes damnées', Baudelaire ends with a bizarre series of images that serve to heighten a misguided championing of the un-championed (stanzas 6-7):

> O demons, monsters, virgins, martyrs, you
> Who trample base reality in scorn,
> Whether as nuns or satyrs you pursue
> The infinite, with cries of tears forlorn,
>
> You, whom my soul has tracked in lairs infernal,
> Poor sisterhood, I pity and adore,
> For your despairing griefs, your thirst eternal,
> And love that floods your hearts for evermore![14]

This poem survived censorship in the republication of *Les Fleurs du mal*; the other two 'lesbian poems' did not. After the 1857 edition, 'Lesbos' and 'Femmes damnées: Delphine et Hippolyte' were two of six poems banned from subsequent editions, after an obscenity trial initiated by the French government. In 1866 Baudelaire published *Les Épaves* (*Scraps*), which incorporated the expurgated poems.

As Baudelaire imagines himself atop 'Leucadia's summit' watching for Sappho's body, his pupil, Swinburne, watches also – both men regarding themselves as the poetic rescuers of her fragmented corpse. Swinburne championed Sappho as 'the very greatest poet that ever lived',[15] and his poem 'Anactoria' is his most famous and infamous homage to her. Echoing the controversy over *Les Fleurs du mal*, the 1866 collection that included 'Anactoria', *Poems and Ballads*, was subject to a ban – although this one was at the instigation of the publisher.

Swinburne's Sappho is the speaker par excellence in 'Anactoria', and her voice is one of sado-masochism of the highest erotic order, as the following excerpt reveals (*ll.* 23-34):

> I would my love could kill thee; I am satiated
> With seeing thee live, and fain would have thee dead.
> I would earth had thy body as fruit to eat,
> And no mouth but some serpent's found thee sweet.
> I would find grievous ways to have thee slain,
> Intense device, and superflux of pain;
> Vex thee with amorous agonies, and shake
> Life at thy lips, and leave it there to ache;
> Strain out thy soul with pangs too soft to kill,

Intolerable interludes, and infinite ill;
Relapse and reluctation of breath,
Dumb tunes and shuddering semitones of death.[16]

Swinburne's Sappho is a harsh mistress of the erotic – domineering, ruthless and possessive (an exaggerated version of Baudelaire's Delphine), yet simultaneously masochistic (her desire to inflict suffering has come from her own suffering). His literary debts – like Baudelaire's – included the Marquis de Sade (1740-1814), whose devotion to sadism was a significant artistic, aesthetic and personal influence on Swinburne's writing and sexuality.

Sadean Sappho continued to appear in the works of Victorian poets, novelists and playwrights,[17] predominantly male, who – one may argue – exploited her perceived sexuality rather than contributed to the salvation of her reputation, free from eroticisation. Additionally, any championing of sexual freedom, particularly that of woman-woman erotics, by poets such as Baudelaire and Swinburne, should be viewed with caution because of their tendency not only to objectify the image of the lesbian but also to relegate her to the position of the 'other'.

Sappho was also painted and sculpted by the Victorians as part of the Sappho vogue. Some of her most notable representations are by the Pre-Raphaelites, most notably by Lawrence Alma-Tadema (1836-1912), whose 'Sappho and Alcaeus' (1881) is among the most celebrated paintings of the School. Symbolist[18] artist Gustave Moreau (1826-1898) was among the leading visionaries when it came to portraits of the poet, producing three major illustrations of her: 'Sappho Leaping from the Leucadian Cliff' (1864), 'The Death of Sappho' (1871) and 'Sappho' (1871). In each small picture – almost icon-like and perfectly executed in watercolour – Moreau's fetish is clearly that part of her story concerning the legendary suicidal leap after Phaon's abandonment. Moreau's Sapphos, one of whom adorns the cover of this book, are excessively ornamental Muses of poetry and despair – exotic, alienated and alienating, defeated yet tragically heroic.

Sappho's point of departure from the mortal world has fascinated many artists in works that range from the trite (the engravings of Anne-Louise Girodet Trison [1927] and William Scott Bell [1873]) to the powerful (Baron Gros' 'Sapho' of 1801) and the unassuming (the undated pen and ink sketch by William Beechey [1753-1839]). The magnitude of the market in suicidal Sapphos is best summarised by Reynolds:

> All over Europe innumerable Sapphos jumped off numberless cliffs, and by the 1790s Sappho Leaping from the Rock of Leucadia became a popular subject for large-scale paintings exhibited at the Paris Salon and the London Royal Academy.[19]

The reasons behind the motif are open to various interpretations and one must, of course, acknowledge the obvious influence of the burgeoning interest in Sappho's poetry (and Classical themes per se) and its multifaceted reinterpretations by Victorian writers. On a less overt, more psychological level, one may posit that such representations of the feminine, be she the idealised, Pre-Raphaelite heroine (perhaps best exemplified by 'Beata Beatrix' [1864-70] by Dante Gabriel Rossetti) or the mythical *femme fatale* (such as Rossetti's 'Pandora' [1869] or his 'Lady Lilith' [1868]), were partly a response to the early developments in women's independence that were to become manifest, for example, in the Women's Emancipation Movement. Feminist scholars argue that the complex gender dichotomies evident in the works of the Pre-Raphaelite Brotherhood, the Decadents and the Symbolists, specifically in their renditions of the female, were partially an anxious response to the New Woman: she who works towards freedom from male control, the bane of the family ideal of the goodly wife and mother.[20]

While Sappho was virtually poised on the brink of death throughout the nineteenth century – and regularly beforehand – she became a positive symbol of the New Woman in the twentieth century when the dawn of feminism began to break and women sought to claim a heritage of their own. With the beginning of Modernism,[21] which is partly characterised by a more respectful reception of women artists, Sappho became an understandable figure or symbol of female representations of their own sexualities, intellectualities and life experiences. Activist, actress and author Elizabeth Robins (1862-1952) refers to Sappho in such roles as 'the nursing mother of intellectually free women',[22] a political interpretation of the poet that was to be significantly developed by Virginia Woolf (1882-1941).[23]

The scholar and Imagist[24] poet H.D. (Hilda Doolittle: 1886-1961) utilised her appreciation of Sappho to express not so much her own bisexuality but a female literary tradition, which she defines in her essay 'The Wise Sappho'. Herein, H.D. utilises Imagist language to encapsulate the effects of Sappho's poetry:

> I think of the words of Sappho as these colours, or states rather, transcending colour yet containing (as great heat the compass of the spectrum) all colour. And perhaps the most

obvious is this rose colour, merging to richer shades of scarlet, purple of Phoenician purple. To the superficial lover – truly – roses![25]

Although conversant in ancient Greek and a proficient translator, H.D. chose not to render Sappho into English but to emulate her in her own, twentieth-century voice. Her poetry is therefore closer to the Roman tradition of imitation, as Diana Collecott notes: 'H.D. embodies actual fragments of Sappho in over thirty poems and embeds many more in her prose.'[26] H.D.'s ability to select the perfect fragment in the perfect poetic context is, according to the strictures of Imagism, to successfully capture the 'part' in the 'whole'.[27]

Like Swinburne, whom she admired, H.D.'s Sappho was one who embraced, fought against and chronicled the deadly powers of the Greek gods, Eros and (as evidenced from the excerpt below) Aphrodite:

Ah no – though I stumble toward
her altar-step,
though my flesh is scorched and rent,
shattered, cut apart,
slashed open;
though my heels press my own wet life
black, dark to purple,
on the smooth rose-streaked
threshold of her pavement.

Thus concludes Part 1 of the poem entitled 'Fragment Forty-one', a piece which, in typical H.D. style, opens with a quotation from Sappho: '… thou flittest to Andromeda.'[28]

6. Debts to Sappho

In the 1970s, *Sappho was a Right-On Woman*, according to Sidney Abbott and Barbara Love in their work subtitled *A Liberated View of Lesbianism*.[29] As the subtitle indicates, this work of non-fiction is more about the lives and struggles of lesbians in the West, predominantly in America, than the poet. Though Sappho gets scant mention except for the title and a poem in the Acknowledgements, her symbolic authority – aura, even – is omnipresent. The book marked a milestone in the reclamation of Sappho in a more unified and wide-spread women-centred environment that combined both art and politics as an expression of liberation and sexuality.

While the image of Sappho was also expanded to encompass free love, celebratory promiscuity and soft porn during the 1960s and 1970s, her role as the Muse of lesbian politics, erotics and literature remained – and remains – constant. Among her most acknowledged poetic successors is Olga Broumas (1949-). Born in Syros, having lived in the United States since 1967, Broumas combines her Greek heritage with contemporary sexual portraits and narratives of a truthful and explicit nature, redolent with evocations such as 'sweet / bruises on her dark skin, her nipples / sucked up like pears' (*Innocence*) and intimacies such as 'Her tits are luminous and sway to the rhythm / and I grab them and exaggerate their orbs' (*She Loves*).[30] In *Sappho's Gymnasium*,[31] written with T. Begley, there is clearly a more overt poetic acknowledgement, although it is the final section of ten, bearing the collection's title, which comes closest to direct Sapphic homage. Here there is a reworking of *fragment* 132:

'I have a young girl good as blossoming gold
her ephemeral face I have formed of a key
dearer than skylark homelands'[32]

141

In recognition of the fragmented condition of the Sapphic corpus, the poets write fragments, each printed on a single page, surrounded by stark white paper – a reminder of what remains and what can be re-visioned. This then is a true reclamation of the Sapphic heritage for modern lesbian artists.

Conclusion

The newly discovered *poem* 58 has been greeted with enthusiasm by the usually staid community of Classicists, and this
animated reception is a reminder of just how fragmentary
the Sapphic corpus is and the precious nature of any addition to it. The reaction recalls the parody of an academic's
response to a new Sapphic fragment in Ronald Firbank's
Vainglory (1915). Professor Inglepin regales his captive audience at a party in honour of the fragment, quoting in Greek,
of course, until someone asks him what it all means – to
which he replies:

> 'In plain English,' the Professor said, with some reluctance,
> 'it means: "Could not" (he wagged a finger) "Could not, for the
> fury of her feet!" '
> 'Do you mean she ran away?'
> 'Apparently!'

The 2004 discovery warrants much more genuine excitement
than the Professor's 'fury of the feet' fragment, although, as
satire often does, Firbank's philological fantasy is a reminder
of how exciting even the smallest discovery can be.

In her lament at growing old, Sappho returns to themes
we have explored throughout this book: the focus on the
condition of the body and its various reactions (*fr.* 31);
beauty (*frr.* 16, 23, 96 and the *epithalamia*); *eros* (*fr.* 130) as
well as divine and mythical themes (*poem* 1, *frr.* 16, 44).

Tithonus is one of the few mortals in Greek mythology to be loved by a goddess and Sappho's fragments further attest her interest in another such youth, Adonis, beloved of Aphrodite. Two fragments are all that remain of Sappho's Adonis:

'He is dying – O Cytherea – pretty Adonis; what are we to do?'
'Beat your breasts, o girls, and tear your garments.' (*fr.* 140[a])

Alas for Adonis! (*fr.* 168)

The tale of Aphrodite and Adonis is well known from various sources. Struck by the beauty of Adonis, Aphrodite fell in love with him and the pair hunted together, but Adonis fell and was gored by a wild boar, leaving the goddess in mourning. Sappho's treatment of the myth is partly homage to the goddess who receives special attention in her poetry and, possibly, her cultic activity on Mytilene. As Stehle suggests: 'The fragment [*fr.* 140(a)] … may be from a cult song, for there was a festival for Adonis celebrated by women, the Adonia.'[1]

Sappho's interest in the theme of goddesses and their mortal lovers may well explain the later 'biographical' connections made between the poet and Phaon. More precisely, Sappho, according to Pseudo-Palaephatus (*c.* fourth century BC), sang about Phaon often.[2] In Chapter 1, the survey of Greek comic poets whose fragments attest the connection between Sappho, Phaon and her famous leap from the Leucadian cliff, did not include Cratinus (450-421 BC), an extant source for love of the ferryman *by Aphrodite herself*. It seems that Cratinus confused this story with that of Adonis, claiming that Sappho hid Phaon in a bed of lettuce, which is a slight variation on the death scene of Adonis, in which Aphrodite also places the dying youth in a bed of lettuce.[3]

Clearly the two male figures of these mythical narratives are easily confused. Both appear to have been the subjects of cult ritual in Mytilene, with Phaon most likely being part of a festival involving Aphrodite that was unique to Lesbos. The confusion of myths, and Sappho's reputation for having sung of both Adonis and Phaon, may well be the key to explaining the origin of Sappho's love of the ferryman and her famous suicidal leap, a legend that was to taint her biography for thousands of years.

Sappho's interest in such tales, besides their cultic relevance, may well have come from their themes of human contact with the divine, something the poet herself dramatises in *poem* 1. The contact is erotic. It is also testimony to the stark and unhappy contrast between divine and human: the gods stay beautiful forever whereas humans age and die. All such themes coalesce in *poem* 58, as Sappho describes her ageing body, introduces the story of Tithonus and, by implication, equates the decay of the body with the departure of *eros* from the life of the individual. As she writes in line 8: 'There is no way, being human, not to grow old.' Perhaps human contact with the divine symbolises for Sappho a glimpse – not only of erotic euphoria – but also immortality.

Since she may have performed some of her own compositions, one can imagine Sappho's rendition of *poem* 58 as dramatic, to say the least. As a solo performance, perhaps with a cithara as accompaniment, the haunting strains and dynamism of the original performance are unrecoverable, as indeed is the audience response. As mentioned in the Introduction, Sappho may have sung her more private songs

– her monodies – at an all-female symposium, namely a gathering of elite women where the participants ate, drank, honoured their deities and, among other activities, recited songs. While scholars have detailed the composition of the ancient male symposium and its various procedures and rituals, there is little material available that sheds light on comparable female gatherings.

Modern comparisons can be unreliable and misleading, yet the temptation to juxtapose antiquity to various facets of contemporary experience is always latent and, at times, scholarly endeavours in such fields have permitted us a glimpse of something we can conceivably relate to the Greeks or Romans. Whether these comparisons bring the ancient experience alive is a matter of academic handling. The field of comparative literature has established ground rules for such practice whereby texts are compared and contrasted, not necessarily for traces of influence, but often for relative explorations of certain themes and artistic techniques.

In Chapter 6 we noted only some of the many artists inspired by Sappho, most of whom were not content to translate or imitate her poetry but sought to re-envision her work – to make it their own – to rewrite it. The identification and examination of this long tradition in literary studies is now an established school of analysis, most commonly known as Reception Theory. It sits beside, yet apart from, Comparative Literary Theory, focusing more on what a new author *does* with an original piece as opposed to tracing similarities. This is not to suggest that Comparative Theory is the more simplistic methodology; indeed it enables a somewhat freer approach to texts that have detectable similarities but without the necessary acknowledgement of detectable literary debt.

With such methodological issues in mind, I would like to end this journey through the world of Sappho with a comparison between her monodies and one of their modern successors: the songs of the torch-singers. Such a comparison is inevitably laid with theoretical booby-traps, but perhaps it may bring us close to a glimpse of Sapphic solo performance.

The first use of the term 'torch-singer' is uncertain but, according to John Moore, the 'torch song's origins are readily apparent'.[4] He continues:

> The song 'Mon Homme' caused a sensation in France just after the First World War. With English lyrics adapted by Channing Pollock, 'My Man' became an instant success in America when presented by Fanny Brice in the 1921 edition of the Ziegfeld Follies, and provided the formula for the torch song.

Admittedly, Fanny Brice and the Ziegfeld Follies are a far cry from Archaic Lesbos and the songs of Sappho, but the development of the torch-song came to recall, in several ways, the pain, anguish and obsessive theme of love (always gone wrong) of the Sapphic corpus.

It is in terms of content, then, that we can detect the sorrows of Sappho's most intimate songs in those of the torch-singer. Traditionally female, the torch-singer, who usually sang other people's songs,[5] lamented unrequited love, ill-treatment at the hands of a male lover, and the state of emotional abandonment. Despite her heartache, the singer still holds a torch for her lover and her torch of fire – her passion – still burns. These images, clearly contributing to the origin of the very words, torch-singer and torch-songs, are as old as Sappho's lyrics; thus we recall *fragment* 31 with its 'soft/ flame' that steals 'beneath' the singer's 'flesh' (*ll.* 9-10) as well as *fragment* 48:

> You came, and I was craving you:
> you cooled my heart, burning with desire.

The torch-singer also sang of the perils of love – a love that sometimes left her on the brink of death. Ella Fitzgerald sang 'Every time we say goodbye, I die a little.' Billie Holiday crooned 'Life's dreary for me.' Libby Holman asked 'Why am I living?'[6] These singers are also on fire: 'I say I'll go through fire/ And I'll go through fire/ As he wants it, so it will be' (Holiday); 'But what a lovely way to burn' (Peggy Lee).[7] The songs of the torch-singer are also bittersweet, best encapsulated by Holiday's version of 'Glad to be Unhappy', particularly the lines: 'But for someone you adore,/ It's a pleasure to be sad' and Ruth Etting's version of 'I'm Good for Nothing but Love', the refrain providing the title of the song.[8]

Performance, the effects of the torch-singer and her songs, was a combination of her visual appearance (her very presence), her voice and the musical accompaniment.[9] The overall effect was exotic and magnetic. Her performances varied each time, with no one rendition the same, the intensity of the experience enhanced by its transitory nature. The power of the performance also lies in the singer's individualistic interpretations of each song and is testimony to the status of singers such as Holiday, Edith Piaf and Marlene Dietrich. As they carefully and melancholically perform each song, spell-binding the audience with the sheer forcefulness of their presence, transforming the joys of love into a form of bitter-sweet suffering, the audience member cannot remain a totally objective observer. The torch-singer's performance thereby gives 'the gift of interpretation'.[10] The torch-singer, in turn, becomes, like Sappho, an icon.

Today, torch-singers write their own songs,[11] and are not always female. The original exoticism and sexual ambiguity of torch singers such as Dietrich have long held appeal as sources of inspiration – both in terms of composition and performance – for male performers, and, particularly female impersonators or drag queens.[12] Indeed complexity of emotion and anguish of love characterise the lyrics and renditions of torch-songs performed in contemporary drag clubs throughout the West – indicative of the importance of the songs of the torch-singers and the women per se in gay culture. While we could trace thematic parallels to Sappho's lyrics in just about every conceivable musical genre, perhaps her legacy is best evidenced today in the torch-songs of gay singer/songwriters. When they sing, some may well detect echoes of Sappho's yearning and sorrow and hope. Reading such lyrics[13] – as opposed to listening to them – is to experience only half the pleasure and the pain, a salient reminder that Sappho composed to be heard. She is, however, very rarely heard today; instead we pore over every fragment that survives on papyrus, paper, even pottery shards. Nevertheless, in the voices of others, her true legacy lives.

Notes

Introduction

1. Pieces of papyri or linen glued together to form sheets that were wrapped round an embalmed body and then decorated.

2. Martin West, 'A New Sappho Poem', *Times Literary Supplement*, June 2005.

3. Germaine Greer, quoted in *The Independent*, October 2005.

4. Greer, 'The Enigma of Sappho', in *Slip-Shod Sibyls: Recognition, Rejection and the Woman Poet* (Viking: 1995) 146. The words are taken from an 1880 letter penned by Algernon Charles Swinburne; see Yopie Prins, *Victorian Sappho* (Princeton University Press: 1999) 115.

5. 'Plato', *Palatine Anthology* 9.506 (= testimonia 60 in D.A. Campbell's *Greek Lyric I: Sappho and Alcaeus*, revised edition [Harvard University Press: 1990]).

6. *Oxyrhynchus Papyrus* 1800 = Campbell testimonia 1.

7. Porphyrion on Horace's *Epistles* = Campbell testimonia 17.

8. See Ellen Greene, 'Introduction', *Women Poets in Ancient Greece and Rome* (University of Oklahoma Press: 2005), especially p. xxi n. 1. See also Ian Plant, *Women Writers of Ancient Greece and Rome* (University of Oklahoma Press: 2004).

9. Greene (2005) xii.

10. The Archaic age (*c.* 800-500 BC).

11. A set of sub-dialects spoken not only in Lesbos, but

150

also in Boeotia in mainland Greece and some of the Greek colonies. Denys Page in *Sappho and Alcaeus: An Introduction to the Study of Ancient Lesbian Poetry* (Clarendon Press: 1955) notes: 'The Aeolic of Sappho and Alcaeus is not a literary dialect; it reflects normal Lesbian usage of the time' (327).

12. A cult name for Aphrodite based on her birth on the island of Cyprus.

13. Lyn Hatherly Wilson, *Sappho's Sweetbitter Songs: Configurations of Female and Male in Ancient Greek Lyric* (Routledge: 1996) 120.

14. André Lardinois, 'Who Sang Sappho's Songs?' in Greene (ed.), *Reading Sappho: Contemporary Approaches* (University of California Press: 1996) 170.

15. Lardinois (1996).

16. Marilyn B. Skinner, *Sexuality in Greek and Roman Culture* (Blackwell: 2005) 60-1.

17. Holt Parker, 'Sappho Schoolmistress', *Transactions and Proceedings of the American Philological Association* 123 (1993) 313. For a refutation of Parker's arguments, see Curtis Bennett, 'Concerning "Sappho Schoolmistress" ', *Transactions and Proceedings of the American Philological Association* 124 (1994) 345-7.

18. See George Saintsbury, ed., *Minor Poets of the Caroline Period* (Clarendon Press: 1905) 493.

19. Ulrich von Wilamowitz-Moellendorf, *Sappho und Simonides* (Weidmann: 1913).

1. Sappho's Lives

1. Bernadette J. Brooten, *Love Between Women: Early Christian Responses to Female Homoeroticism* (University of Chicago Press: 1996) 34.

2. Lardinois, 'Lesbian Sappho and Sappho of Lesbos' in Jan Bremmer (ed.), *From Sappho to De Sade: Moments in the History of Sexuality* (Routledge: 1989) 22.

3. Menander, *fragment* 258; see Strabo, *Geography* 10.2.9 = Campbell testimonia 23.

4. *Suda*, 'Sappho', Second Notice = Campbell testimonia 3.

5. Translations of Ovid are by Terry Ryan (University of Newcastle: 2006).

6. Greer (1995) 123.

7. Quoted by Harriette Andreadis in *Sappho in Early Modern Europe: Female Same-Sex Literary Erotics 1550-1714* (University of Chicago Press: 2001) 31.

8. *Suda*, 'Sappho', First Notice = Campbell testimonia 2.

9. See Campbell 5 n. 4.

10. Scholars have questioned the validity of assuming that Cleis is Sappho's daughter, noting that the word used for 'child', *pais*, does not specifically denote an offspring. However, the additional word, *agapetos*, translated above as 'precious', means 'that with which one must be content', and can therefore denote an only child.

11. Herodotus, *Histories* 2.135 and Strabo, *Geography* 17.1.33 = Campbell text 202. See also *Oxyrhynchus Papyrus* 1800: '… she had three brothers, Erigyius, Larichus [the youngest] and Charaxus: the eldest one sailed to Egypt and became acquainted with a woman called Doricha, spending considerable money on her.'

12. *Hetaira* (singular)/ *hetairai* (plural) also means 'courtesan/ courtesans', although clearly not in this context. There was, however, yet another tradition from antiquity that claimed Sappho to be a prostitute.

13. Maximus of Tyre, *Orations* 18.9 = Campbell testi-

monia 20. See also Plutarch who makes the same comparison in *Moralia: The Oracles at Delphi* 406A.

14. Dionysius of Halicarnassus, *On Literary Composition* 23 (part of which is included in Campbell as text 11). For the complete text see Stephen Usher's translation (Harvard University Press: 1985).

15. Longinus, *On the Sublime* 10.1-3 = Campbell text 31.

16. Margaret Reynolds, *The Sappho Companion* (Vintage: 2001) 18.

17. Andreadis 37.

18. See Brooten 33 n. 19.

19. Joan DeJean, *Fictions of Sappho, 1546-1937* (University of Chicago Press: 1989) 1.

20. Greer (1995) 132.

21. See DeJean 57.

22. See DeJean 59.

23. DeJean 56.

24. Quoted by Andreadis 29.

25. Quoted by Greer (1995) 126.

26. Christine de Pisan, *The Book of the City of Ladies*, translated by Earle Jeffrey Richards, quoted by Reynolds (2001) 87. An English edition of the French text first appeared in 1521.

27. *Oxyrhynchus Papyrus* 1800 = Campbell testimonia 1. Obviously the discovery of this specific passage was well after de Pisan's lifetime; nevertheless it is an effective and concise example of the negative representations of Sappho's appearance, others of which de Pisan may have read.

28. See n. 27.

29. From Jane McIntosh Snyder, 'Sappho in Attic Vase Painting', in Ann Olga Koloski-Ostrow and Claire L. Lyons (eds), *Naked Truths: Women, Sexuality, and Gender in Classical Art and Archaeology* (Routledge: 1997a) 108.

30. *The Complete Poems of Emily Dickinson* (Little, Brown, and Company: 1924).

31. Parker, 'Sappho's Public World', in Greene (2005) 3.

32. Parian Marble = Campbell testimonia 5.

33. For discussion of the political situation on Mytilene during Sappho's time, see Oswyn Murray, *Early Greece* (Fontana: 1980) 148-52; Anthony J. Podlecki, *The Early Greek Poets and their Times* (University of British Columbia Press: 1984) 62-88 (especially 82-8). See also Page duBois, *Sappho is Burning* (University of Chicago Press: 1995) 5-6.

34. Parker (2005) 6. Alcaeus refers to the house of Penthilus in *fragments* 70 and 75 (in Campbell).

2. Songs for the Gods

1. From Marguerite Johnson and Terry Ryan, *Sexuality in Greek and Roman Society and Literature: A Sourcebook* (Routledge: 2005) 27. Other Sapphic fragments are cited therein, notably the marriage hymns, although most have slight variations.

2. The term 'Indo-European' was coined to denote the Indo-European language group (initially confined to the area between and encompassing India and Europe); its meaning developed to collectively define the cultures associated with these languages. It is hypothesised that these cultures arose from the expansion of an ancient people, the Proto-Indo-Europeans, whose origin has been most commonly suggested as either Russia or Anatolia.

3. The first known Greek script, Linear B was recorded on tablets dating from the fourteenth and thirteenth centuries BC.

4. Homer, *Iliad* 5.370-1.

5. Hesiod, *Theogony* 188-206. Hesiod, from Cyme in Aeolis, migrated to Ascra in Greece. His two major works are *Theogony*, an account of the creation of the world, and *Works and Days*, a farming manual that includes various anecdotes about the gods, Greek folklore and advice on topics that extend beyond agriculture.

6. For an alternative and persuasive reading, see Anne Carson, 'The Justice of Aphrodite in Sappho 1', in Greene (1996) 226-32. Carson presents an argument, based on the absence of a direct object for the verbs of lines 21-4 (hence the square parentheses in the translation), that Aphrodite's justice will take the form of causing the woman, sometime in the future, to experience rejected love (just like Sappho).

7. See Leah Rissman, *Love as War: Homeric Allusion in the Poetry of Sappho* (Hain: 1983).

8. *Iliad* 18.389f.; *Odyssey* 19.55f.

9. Page 5.

10. See Chapter 3 for more on this story.

11. *c.* fifth-fourth centuries BC.

12. See Kenneth Dover, *Greek Homosexuality* (Duckworth: 1978); Daniel H. Garrison, *Sexual Culture in Ancient Greece* (University of Oklahoma Press: 2000); Johnson and Ryan.

13. Skinner (2005) 59.

14. From the mid first century BC onwards.

15. Margaret Williamson, *Sappho's Immortal Daughters* (Harvard University Press: 1995) 57.

16. Jack Winkler, 'Double Consciousness in Sappho's Lyrics', in *Constraints of Desire: The Anthropology of Sex and Gender in Ancient Greece* (Routledge: 1990) 186.

17. See H.G. Evelyn-White's *Hesiod, The Homeric Hymns and The Homerica* (Harvard University Press: 1913). The *Cypria*, a fragmentary work of uncertain date, although

roughly contemporaneous with the Homeric epics, appears to have been a narration of the events preceding the Trojan War including the argument between Achilles and Agamemnon, which opens the *Iliad*.

18. See M. Eleanor Irwin, 'Roses and the Bodies of Beautiful Women', *Echos du Monde / Classical Views* 38.13 (1994) 1-13 (especially p. 12).

19. Eugene Stock McCarthy, 'How the Apple Became the Token of Love', *Transactions and Proceedings of the American Philological Association* 56 (1925) 70-81 (p. 70).

20. Winkler 108 (italics added).

21. Judith P. Hallett, 'Sappho and Her Social Context: Sense and Sensuality' in Greene (1996) 141. My reading of this topic has been informed by Lardinois' 'Who Sang Sappho's Songs?' in Greene (1996) 150-72.

22. An interpretation essentially based on a comparative reading of Sappho's *fragment* 17 and Alcaeus' *fragment* 129.

23. God of fertility, wine and the release of inhibitions, Dionysus was of particular appeal to Greek women. His most famous literary representation was in Euripides' tragedy, *Bacchae* (405 BC).

24. See, for example, Wilson, whose work has been inspired by French feminist linguists such as Luce Irigaray, Julia Kristeva and Helene Cixous (15-18). Skinner, whose research is also inspired by this French school, offers a more balanced reading of the female voice in Sapphic lyrics; see 'Women and Language in Archaic Greece, or, Why Is Sappho a Woman?' in Greene (1996) 175-92.

25. See E. Lobel and Denys Page, 'A New Fragment of Aeolic Verse', *Classical Quarterly* 2 (1952) 1-3.

26. Cited above as one of Sappho's fragments on the Muses.

27. Page 261.

28. G.M. Kirkwood, *Early Greek Monody: The History of a Poetic Type* (Cornell University Press: 1974) 145-6.

29. Kirkwood 146. Like Kirkwood, Page (69), albeit guardedly, attributes 44A to Sappho.

3. Mythical Lyrics

1. Jane McIntosh Snyder, *Lesbian Desire in the Lyrics of Sappho* (Columbia University Press: 1997b) 74.

2. Page 67.

3. Page 71.

4. Page. In agreement is C.M. Bowra, *Greek Lyric Poetry* (Harvard University Press: 1961) 231.

5. Most recently, Williamson 75.

6. For the purposes of convenience, the name 'Hesiod' is used.

7. An epithet derived from Ilus, the founder of Troy.

8. See Wilson 150-7; Eva Stehle, *Performance and Gender in Ancient Greece: Nondramatic Poetry in its Setting* (Princeton University Press: 1997) 278-9.

9. Despite the fragmentary nature of the piece, with a gap 'of indeterminable length' (Page 70), each time there is a resumption of narrative, it is still on the mythic theme without any reference to an actual wedding ceremony.

10. See Chapter 2 n. 29.

11. H. Fränkel, *Early Greek Poetry and Philosophy*, trans. M. Hadas (Oxford University Press: 1975) 187.

12. This interpretation is indebted to G.W. Most's article, 'Sappho Fr. 16.6-7 L-P', *Classical Quarterly* 31 (1981) 11-17. Most states: 'Some ... have seen in παράγειν [*paragein*] (11) an implicit condemnation of Helen's action. This is not quite accurate. In archaic Greek lyric (the word does not occur in

Homer or Hesiod), παράγω [*paragô*] describes the way a non-rational force interferes with one's purposively calculating intellect, irresistibly diverting … one from the intended goal to others' (16 n. 32).

13. For an alternative reading, see Paul Allen Miller, *Lyric Texts and Lyric Consciousness: The Birth of a Genre from Archaic Greece to Augustan Rome* (Routledge: 1994) 92-6.

14. There are instances in the Homeric epics where Achilles (*Iliad* 19.324-5) and Eumaeus, the swineherd (*Odyssey* 14.67-71) blame Helen. Inevitably, however, such outbursts are based on context: Achilles reacts against her during his despair over the death of his closest friend, Patroclus, while Eumaeus is disgruntled at the absence of his master, Odysseus, and the hardship this has caused him. The role of Aphrodite in Helen's departure for Troy is most strongly suggested in Book 3 of the *Iliad* where the goddess appears to her and demands she visit the bedchamber of Paris (*ll.* 390-4); Helen attempts to defy her but is threatened and eventually succumbs to her order.

15. Page 280.

16. These interpretations have been influenced by William H. Race, 'Sappho *Fr.* 16 L-P and Alkaios *Fr.* 42 L-P: Romantic and Classical Strains in Lesbian Lyric', *Classical Journal* 85 (1989) 16-33 (p. 23).

17. Garrison 74.

4. Love of Women

1. The Greek comic playwright Aristophanes (*c.* 448 – *c.* 385 BC) provides the earliest extant usage of the verb. In his plays *lesbiazein* is used in a heterosexual context in relation to a woman 'using the mouth / tongue' on a male. See Jeffrey

Henderson, *The Maculate Muse: Obscene Language in Attic Comedy*, 2nd edn (Oxford University Press: 1991) 183-4.

2. Such a reputation may have come from comic vituperation on the part of the Athenians during their conflict with the Mytileneans in the sixth century BC (Dover 183).

3. Hallett 130.

4. Plutarch, *Lycurgus*: 'though this love [male-to-male] was so approved among them that also the noble and good women loved virgins, there was no jealous love in it' (18.4).

5. The *Theognidea* defines those pieces from the works of the poet Theognis of Megara that are in dispute as to authorship.

6. See Dover 179-80.

7. Anne Pippin Burnett, *Three Archaic Poets: Archilochus, Alcaeus, Sappho* (Harvard University Press: 1983) 226.

8. See Snyder (1997b) 32-5; attention is also given to allusions to the *Odyssey*, particularly Odysseus' speech to Nausicaa (*Odyssey* 6.158-61).

9. This translation of Catullus is by Terry Ryan (University of Newcastle: 2006).

10. The final stanza of *poem* 51 has caused problems for editors of the Catullan manuscript for nothing resembles it in what remains of the Sapphic original. This has led some scholars to argue that the stanza in fact belongs to another poem and had been misplaced by scribes. The argument concerning the placement of lines 13-16 is further complicated by the badly preserved final stanza of *fragment* 31, which translate as follows: 'But all can be suffered, since … yet a poor man …' (*l.* 17). This may have originally formed the equivalent of the final lines of *poem* 51 (available in the first century BC) or, alternatively, Catullus may have decided to make the original his own by the inclusion of a different ending.

11. *Iliad* 9.128-30.

12. Wilamowitz 58.

13. Bruno Snell, 'Sapphos Gedicht *phainetai moi kenos*', *Hermes* 66 (1931) 71-90.

14. Although one of the most thorough analyses is earlier, see George L. Koniaris, 'On Sappho, Fr. 31 (L-P)', *Philologus* 112 (1968) 173-86. Prior to Koniaris, Page (31-3) also questioned the interpretation. For a concise analysis, see Snyder (1997b) 29-31.

15. Page 32.

16. Koniaris 173.

17. Page 33; Page also cites Plutarch's *Dialogue on Love*, 763.

18. For an argument in favour of the woman as the speaker, see Anne Burnett, 'Desire and Memory (Sappho Frag. 94)', *Classical Philology* 74 (1979) 16-27; for a contrary interpretation, see Thomas McEvilley, 'Sappho, Fragment Ninety-Four', *Phoenix* 25 (1971) 1-11 and Emmet Robbins, 'Who's Dying in Sappho Fr. 94?' *Phoenix* 44 (1990) 111-21.

19. Greene, 'Sappho, Foucault, and Women's Erotics', *Arethusa* 29 (1996) 9.

20. From McEvilley 2-3.

21. McEvilley 3.

22. A third piece, *fragment* 95, was also included on the same parchment.

23. For a discussion, see Rebecca Hague, 'Sappho's Consolation for Atthis, fr. 96 L-P', *American Journal of Philology* 105 (1984) 29-36 (especially pp. 29-31).

24. Hague 30.

25. The Greek botanical noun, *anthruskon*, has not been conclusively identified; besides 'cow-parsley', 'melilot' has been suggested.

26. There are alternative accounts of Herse's parentage; see H.J. Rose, *A Handbook of Greek Mythology*, 6th edn (Methuen: 1958) 110-11.

27. G.O. Hutchinson, *Greek Lyric Poetry: A Commentary on Selected Larger Pieces* (Oxford University Press: 2001) 182.

28. See Chapter 1, n. 8.

29. See also Chapter 1.

30. Eva-Maria Voigt, *Sappho et Alcaeus: Fragmenta* (Athenaeum-Polak and Van Gennep: 1971) 131.

31. Plutarch, *Dialogue on Love* = Campbell text 49.

32. J.C.B. Petropoulos, 'Sappho the Sorceress – Another Look at Fr. 1 (LP)', *Zeitschrift für Papyrologie und Epigraphik* 97 (1993) 56. Petropoulos acknowledges the work of previous scholars in this analysis.

33. Petropoulos 49.

34. Petropoulos.

35. See Petropoulos 43 n. 4.

36. Snyder (1997b) 69.

37. Skinner (2005) 57.

38. Skinner, 'Aphrodite Garlanded: *Erôs* and Poetic Creativity in Sappho and Nossis', in Nancy Sorkin Rabinowitz and Lisa Auanger (eds), *Among Women: From the Homosocial to the Homoerotic in the Ancient World* (University of Texas Press: 2002) 66.

39. Stehle, 'Sappho's Gaze: Fantasies of a Goddess and Young Man', in Greene (1996) 220.

40. Composed between 360 and 355 BC.

41. Athenaeus (= Campbell text 138) introduces the quotation accordingly: 'And Sappho says to a man who is exceedingly admired for his physique and considered beautiful ...' (564d).

5. *Marriage Hymns*

1. Charles Segal, 'Eros and Incantation: Sappho and Oral Poetry', in Greene (1996) 71.

2. In this instance, owing to Peleus' dispossession, Thetis is escorted to the land of the centaur, Chiron (Peleus' defender and surrogate father), in Thessaly. It will be here that Chiron will raise the offspring of Peleus and Thetis, Achilles.

3. *Parthenos* refers not only to a virgin (or, simply, a girl) but also designates, socially, an unmarried female. On this term, Williamson writes: 'The status of parthenos is linked with sexuality in two ways. It is defined in terms of sexual relations, denoting the stage of life preceding marriage; and it has erotic connotations' (119).

4. In addition to the works of Hesiod, see Semonides *Poem* 7 (seventh century BC).

5. While consensus is in favour of the marriage context, which is the principal reason for the inclusion of the piece in this chapter, I draw attention to the word *pais*, which is usually translated as 'child' (of either sex), but here translated as 'boy'. The use here reflects the poet's ability to capture the thoughts of a very young girl. It is also used by Theocritus (*Idyll* 18.13) to describe the bride Helen by her female peers; see Johnson and Ryan 73 n. 6.

6. See Chapter 4.

7. Skinner (1996) 186.

8. Demetrius, *On Style* 167 = Campbell text 110(b).

9. Page 120.

10. Williamson 81.

11. See Johnson and Ryan 71-3.

12. On Hesiod, see Chapter 2, n. 4.

13. Stobaeus, *Anthology* 4.22.112.

14. Syrianus 1.15.
15. *On Style* 106.
16. See n. 13.
17. Ancient poets did compare female virginity with flowers; see, for example, Archilochus' *Cologne Epode* (*ll.* 26-7) and, less emphatic in direct equation, the *Homeric Hymn to Gaia* (*ll.* 14-15).
18. The translations of Catullus' *poem* 62 are by Terry Ryan (University of Newcastle: 2006).
19. E.S. Stigers, 'Retreat from the Male: Catullus 62 and Sappho's Erotic Flowers', *Ramus* 6 (1977) 96.
20. See Snyder (1997b) 107-8 (including a brief discussion that draws attention to one other scholarly theory).
21. See n. 5.

6. Debts to Sappho

1. Translated by Terry Ryan (University of Newcastle: 2006).
2. D.A. Campbell, 'Aeolian Carmen: Horace's Allusions to Sappho and Alcaeus', *Echos du Monde Classique* 22 (1978) 95.
3. See Horace's *Satire* 55.193. Scholars have also identified *imitatio* of Sappho's *fragment* 90 in Horace's *Carmina* 3.12.
4. Reynolds (2001) 73.
5. Michael Field, *Works and Days: From the Journal of Michael Field*, T. and D.C. Sturge Moore, eds (John Murray: 1933) in Prins 76.
6. Prins 74.
7. For a lively survey, see Reynolds (2001) 262-3.
8. Louÿs' *Les Chansons de Bilitis*, John Keats (1795-1821), Charles Baudelaire (1821-1867) and Swinburne (1837-1909).

9. Reynolds (2001) 291.

10. See Reynolds (2003) 148-68.

11. William Aggeler, trans., *The Flowers of Evil* (Academy Library Guild: 1954).

12. Originally a term coined in hostility, 'Decadent' became a literary definition of a category of artists of the nineteenth century who rejected the idealism of nature as espoused by the Romantic poets and promoted the concept of original sin and humanity's predilection for the flesh, for evil, for desires far from the aesthetics of innocence.

13. Aggeler.

14. Roy Campbell, trans., *Poems of Baudelaire* (Pantheon Books: 1952).

15. In a letter dated 1880; from Prins 115 (see also Introduction, n. 4). For an analysis of Swinburne's Sappho, see Prins 112-73.

16. Swinburne, *Poems and Ballads* (J.C. Hotten: 1866); see also Kenneth Haynes's edition, *Poems and Ballads & Atalanta in Calydon* (Penguin: 2000).

17. See Reynolds (2001) 232-3.

18. The Symbolists were closely aligned with the Decadents and drew their inspiration from Baudelaire, particularly his *Les Fleurs du mal*. Like the Decadents, the Symbolists were in search of new modes of expression and therefore returned to Classical and biblical themes, which they reinterpreted through the lens of surrealism and the subconscious, especially the world of dreams.

19. Reynolds (2003) 68.

20. See Reynolds (2003) 68-76.

21. The Modernist movement was defined by its acceptance – indeed embracement – of the technological, urban and scientific developments of the twentieth century. With

its philosophical heritage in nineteenth-century France, Modernism sought to match artistic endeavour and productivity with the industrial qualities of twentieth-century society and its devotees aimed, in part, at capturing a more concise, indeed abstract, representation of subject in art, music and literature. Sigmund Freud (1856-1939) was an influential force on the movement, with his revelatory psychological theories on the unconscious and the tension between subconscious desires and social restrictions producing an important new means of expressing the complexities of emotions in artistic language.

22. Elizabeth Robins, *Ancilla's Share: An Indictment of Sex Antagonism* (1924; Hyperion: 1976), first published anonymously.

23. See, for example, Reynolds' concise overview (2003: 231-7).

24. A movement instigated by American and English poets, predominantly Ezra Pound (1885-1972), H.D. and her husband, Richard Aldington (1892-1962) in *c.* 1912. The Imagists were descendants of the Symbolists (see above, n. 18) and, like them, sought to reject the style of the Romantics, preferring concrete imagery, economy of language, experimental structure and a return to the themes of Classicism.

25. H.D., *Notes on Thoughts and Vision & The Wise Sappho* (City Lights Books: 1982) 57. The essay was thought to have been written *c.* 1919, but was not published until 1982.

26. Diana Collecott, *H.D. and Sapphic Modernism 1910-1950* (Cambridge University Press: 1999) 10.

27. See Collecott 11.

28. H.D., *Heliodora and Other Poems* (Jonathan Cape: 1924).

29. Sidney Abbott and Barbara Love, *Sappho was a Right-On Woman: A Liberated View of Lesbianism* (Stein and Day: 1972).

30. Olga Broumas, *Beginning with O* (Yale University Press: 1977) and *Perpetua* (Copper Canyon Press: 1989), respectively.

31. Broumas and T. Begley, *Sappho's Gymnasium* (Copper Canyon Press: 1994).

32. Broumas and Begley 172. The reference to 'key' is a pun on the literal meaning of the name Cleis (Key).

Conclusion

1. Stehle, 'Sappho's Gaze: Fantasies of a Goddess and Young Man', in Greene 195.

2. Pseudo-Palaephatus, *On Incredible Events* = Campbell testimonia 211(a).

3. See Campbell, testimonia 211(b)[i] and 211(b)[ii].

4. John Moore, ' "The hieroglyphics of love": the torch singers and interpretation', *Popular Music* 8 (1989) 31.

5. Thus there are multiple versions of the same song by various singers.

6. 'Every Time We Say Goodbye' (Porter); 'Body and Soul' (Green/ Heyman/ Sour/ Eyton); 'Why Was I Born?' (Kern and Hammerstein).

7. 'Crazy He Calls Me' (Sigman/ Russell); 'Fever' (Lee).

8. 'Glad to be Unhappy' (Hart and Rodgers); 'I'm Good for Nothing but Love' (Maltin and Ballard).

9. From Moore 33.

10. Moore 55.

11. John Potter, 'The singer, not the song: women singers as composer-poets', *Popular Music* 13 (1994) 191-9.

12. Best represented in Harvey Fierstein's *Torch Song Trilogy* (1988), a film directed by Paul Bogart, based on Fierstein's stage to screen script.

13. See p. 8 for excerpts from two songs by Antony and the Johnsons that capture the sentiments of the Sapphic singer.

Select Bibliography

Editions of Sappho

Campbell, D.A. (ed. & trans.), *Greek Lyric I: Sappho and Alcaeus*, revised edn (Harvard University Press: 1990). The poems appear in both Greek and English.

Carson, Anne, *If Not, Winter: Fragments of Sappho* (Knopf: 2002; Virago: 2003). The poems appear in both Greek and English, followed by Notes, Who's Who and an Appendix on some testimonia.

Page, Denys, *Sappho and Alcaeus: An Introduction to the Study of Ancient Lesbian Poetry* (Clarendon Press: 1955). Selected poems appear in both Greek and English. The commentary is aimed primarily at readers of ancient Greek.

West, M.L. (trans.), *Greek Lyric Poetry* (Oxford University Press: 1994). Translations of early Greek poetry, including Sappho, from the seventh to the fifth centuries BC.

Scholarly works on Sappho

Bennett, Curtis, 'Concerning "Sappho Schoolmistress" ', *Transactions and Proceedings of the American Philological Association* 124 (1994) 345-7.

Brooten, B.J., *Love Between Women: Early Christian Responses to Female Homoeroticism* (University of Chicago Press: 1996).

duBois, P., 'Sappho and Helen', in *Women in the Ancient World: The Arethusa Papers,* ed. J. Peradotto and J.P.

Sullivan. (State University of New York Press: 1984) 95-105.

———, *Sappho is Burning* (University of Chicago Press: 1995).

Greene, Ellen (ed.), *Reading Sappho: Contemporary Approaches* (University of California Press: 1996).

———, 'Sappho, Foucault, and Women's Erotics', *Arethusa* 29 (1996) 1-14.

——— (ed.), *Women Poets in Ancient Greece and Rome* (University of Oklahoma Press: 2005).

Greer, Germaine, 'The Enigma of Sappho', in *Slip-Shod Sibyls: Recognition, Rejection and the Woman Poet* (Viking: 1995).

Hallett, J.P. 'Sappho and Her Social Context: Sense and Sensuality', *Signs* 4 (1979) 447-64.

Lardinois, André, 'Lesbian Sappho and Sappho of Lesbos', in *From Sappho to De Sade: Moments in the History of Sexuality*, ed. Jan Bremmer (Routledge: 1989).

Parker, Holt, 'Sappho Schoolmistress', *Transactions and Proceedings of the American Philological Association* 123 (1993) 309-51.

Plant, Ian, *Women Writers of Ancient Greece and Rome* (University of Oklahoma Press: 2004).

Rissman, Leah, *Love as War: Homeric Allusion in the Poetry of Sappho* (Hain: 1983).

Skinner, Marilyn B., 'Women and Language in Ancient Greece, or, Why is Sappho a Woman?', in *Feminist Theory and the Classics*, ed. Nancy Sorkin Rabinowitz and Amy Richlin (Routledge: 1993) 125-44.

Snyder, Jane McIntosh, 'Sappho in Attic Vase Painting', in *Naked Truths: Women, Sexuality and Gender in Classical Art and Archaeology*, ed. Ann Olga Koloski-Ostrow and Claire L. Lyons (Routledge: 1997a).

————, *Lesbian Desire in the Lyrics of Sappho* (Columbia University Press: 1997b).

Stigers, E.S., 'Retreat from the Male: Catullus 62 and Sappho's Erotic Flowers', *Ramus* 6 (1977) 83-102.

Williamson, Margaret, *Sappho's Immortal Daughters* (Harvard University Press: 1995).

Wilson, L.H., *Sappho's Sweetbitter Songs: Configurations of Female and Male in Ancient Greek Lyric* (Routledge: 1996).

Winkler, J., 'Double Consciousness in Sappho's Lyrics', in *Constraints of Desire: The Anthropology of Sex and Gender in Ancient Greece* (Routledge: 1990) 162-87.

Supplementary reading: ancient gender and sexuality

Blundell, S., *Women in Ancient Greece* (British Museum Press: 1995).

Cantarella, E., *Pandora's Daughters: The Role and Status of Women in Greek and Roman Antiquity*, trans. M.B. Fant (Johns Hopkins University Press: 1987).

————, *Bisexuality in the Ancient World*, trans. C. Ó Cuilleanáin (Yale University Press: 1992).

Dover, K.J., *Greek Homosexuality* (Duckworth: 1978).

Foucault, M., *The History of Sexuality*, vol. 1: *An Introduction*, trans. R. Hurley (Penguin: 1978).

————, *The History of Sexuality*, vol. 2: *The Use of Pleasure*, trans. R. Hurley (Penguin: 1985).

Daniel H. Garrison, *Sexual Culture in Ancient Greece* (University of Oklahoma Press: 2000).

Johnson, Marguerite and Terry Ryan, *Sexuality in Greek and Roman Society and Literature: A Sourcebook* (Routledge: 2005).

Skinner, Marilyn B., *Sexuality in Greek and Roman Culture* (Blackwell: 2005).

Supplementary reading: Sappho in post-antiquity

Andreadis, Harriette, *Sappho in Early Modern Europe: Female Same-Sex Literary Erotics 1550-1714* (University of Chicago Press: 2001).

DeJean, Joan, *Fictions of Sappho, 1546-1937* (University of Chicago Press: 1989).

Guber, Susan, 'Sapphistries', *Signs* 10 (1984) 43-62.

Prins, Yopie, *Victorian Sappho* (Princeton University Press: 1999).

Reynolds, Margaret, *The Sappho Companion* (Vintage: 2001).

————, *The Sappho History* (Palgrave: 2003).

Index

Index